HOW TO WRITE SONGS THAT $ELL

L. PERRY WILBUR

HOW TO WRITE SONGS THAT $ELL

L. PERRY WILBUR

Henry Regnery Company•Chicago

Library of Congress Cataloging in Publication Data

Wilbur, L. Perry
  How to write songs that sell.

    1. Music, Popular (Songs, etc.)—Writing and
publishing.   I. Title.
MT67.W718   784'.028   76-55653
ISBN 0-8092-7861-8
ISBN 0-8092-7846-4 (pbk.)

Published by Henry Regnery Company
180 North Michigan Avenue, Chicago, Illinois 60601
Manufactured in the United States of America
Library of Congress Catalog Card Number: 76-55653
International Standard Book Number: 0-8092-7861-8 (cloth)
                                0-8092-7846-4 (paper)
Published simultaneously in Canada by
Beaverbooks
953 Dillingham Road
Pickering, Ontario L1W 1Z7
Canada

To my parents, who have often
given me credit for many hit songs

Contents

Preface

This book is meant for you, for anyone and everyone who ever dreamed of making a fortune as a songwriter. It's intended to show you how to create, write, compose, protect, market, and promote original songs.

From his meteoric rise as a recording artist in the mid-1950s, Elvis Presley is a good example of how far one can go in the fabulous music industry. The king of rock and roll has retained his glamour, and his legend continues. A private road beside his Graceland mansion now provides extra room for the lineup of cars and thousands of fans who come from everywhere to see his home and to get a glimpse of the superstar himself.

But the recording artist of any era would have to close up shop without songwriters to write their new material. It's the songwriters who keep the music industry humming and make the world a happier place.

Whether you make a million dollars on your songs or

not, there's a world of satisfaction and creative adventure waiting for you as a part-time or full-time songwriter. This book tells you how to place the songs you write and promote them before and after they are recorded.

You will discover in the pages of this book what it takes to write a hit song. And who knows? A hit of tomorrow may have your name on it.

This book can guide and inspire you along the way . . . as the one who writes the lyrics, the music, or both. And remember, whether they're writing for profit or pleasure, songwriters always have more fun.

HOW TO WRITE SONGS THAT $ELL

L. PERRY WILBUR

1

Song Ideas Are Everywhere

How would you like to see your name on new records being sold all over the country, even all over the world—your name as the songwriter? Would you enjoy hearing your songs played on radio stations and sung by leading recording artists? This book can help you make your dreams come true.

Even if the songs you bring to life are never placed with publishers and are never recorded, you can still have a wonderful time writing them and playing or singing them for your own pleasure. Your family and friends will also enjoy hearing them. Dreaming up new songs—actually creating them from nothing but an idea—is one of the most interesting leisure-time activities of all. It's highly creative, stimulating, and lots of fun, too. And there's always the chance your songs will make money.

According to conservative estimates, some twenty million or more Americans from all walks of life are trying to write songs that will earn money. Millions more are writing for the pure fun of it. The huge number of those striving for commercial success includes teenagers, servicemen, teachers, students in college with an interest in music, businessmen, professional people, people of all ages.

All of them at one time or another—for the enjoyment of it, or on the chance that their songs might make money—have caught the songwriting bug. Writing songs is in their blood, and they love it. Most of them keep writing whether their songs sell or not. The odds are against their coming up with a hit, or getting that hit launched and recorded, and they know it. But millions of them get a world of pleasure out of just kicking new ideas around and creating new songs. Songwriting offers them a marvelous creative hobby, along with the thrilling expectation that one of their songs may be recorded, and even go on to become a smash hit.

How This Book Can Help You

Whether you're a beginner with only an interest in songwriting, someone more experienced or who has already written lyrics, melodies, or complete songs, or a veteran with years of songs behind you, this book will help you. You will learn how to get ideas for songs, how to write lyrics and melodies, how to find a collaborator if you write only the words or tunes, how to polish and improve what you've written, how to protect your completed song, what a copyright really means, and why you should copyright only certain songs.

For leisure-time enjoyment and/or possible profit, this book will guide you as to what to do with your finished songs, how to get a demonstration recording of your song, what to do with the demo, how to contact publishers, record companies, and artists about your song, what it takes for a hit, how to choose the type music where you stand the best chance, how to promote your material, and how to specialize in the kind of songs that interest you the most.

You'll find some chapters in this book on the world of country music, on the opportunities in this category of music, on the vivid realness of today's country songs, and on Roger Miller's rise to writing and singing success.

You'll learn in Chapter 22 about the almost mystical way that one writer's unique career got started. You'll see how he decided to specialize in writing lyrics and stuck to it, going on to carve a brilliant career as a Hollywood motion picture lyricist. He will tell you how he writes his international hit songs, what it was like to win three different best song-of-the-year motion picture academy Oscars, his opinion of the music of the future, and incredibly, how one of his greatest hits, "Love Is a Many-Splendored Thing," was turned down by five major artists, though it later went on to become a giant international standard and won an Academy Award.

Above all, you will discover first-hand in this book how much fun you can have once you learn how to create your own songs. The chapter on some of the all-time famous songwriters—Gershwin, Berlin, Kern, Cole Porter, and others —is bound to inspire you.

Don't miss out on the world of creative satisfaction, fun, and possible profit awaiting you in the world of songwriting. The pages of this book will open the songwriting portals to you and guide you along the way. There's a place for you in songwriting. And who knows? You may well come up with one of tomorrow's smash hit songs. If you don't, you're still in for the time of your life as a creative songwriter. The next section will show you how to begin.

Ideas for Songs Are All Around You

Ideas for new songs are literally everywhere. You can find them by simply walking around and observing what happens to you and your friends, on vacation or on the job wherever you work or play. One huge source for ideas is in the vast amount of reading material available to you now. Good song ideas often can leap out at you from the pages of books, magazines, or newspapers, from weather reports, verses, humorous material, and even textbooks. The greater variety of material you read the better.

Reading Triggers Your Imagination

The act of reading will stimulate your imagination. The more ideas you produce, the better chance you have of coming up with a blockbuster. And one great song idea is sometimes all you need.

Above all, when you run across a good idea for a new song be sure to get it down on paper as soon as possible. A newspaper story, actually a weather report, triggered the mind of Harry Von Tilzer and led him to write one of his greatest hits, "Wait Til the Sun Shines, Nellie." This same process of finding ideas is happening now to today's writers. The weather report Von Tilzer read told about an unfortunate family on New York's East Side, and the journalist predicted that after the storm had passed the sun would shine. Von Tilzer's mind, trained to be alert for song ideas, instantly leaped on this idea, added the name, Nellie, and the result was a smash hit song.

Inspiration from Personal Tragedy

Years ago, shortly after a young woman named Ruth Lowe married, her husband, a handsome young pianist, suddenly died. Ruth, who was far from her home in Toronto, was left to face the future alone. The piano her husband had loved so much (and which she too had loved, because of him) now remained silent because the sound of it reminded her so much of him. But one night this grief-stricken young Canadian decided to rechannel her grief and heartsickness into the words and music of a song.

The beautiful melody and touching words Ruth wrote that night were well blended by the driving force of her love turned to grief. She succeeded in what she tried to do that night. The song she wrote was, "I'll Never Smile Again," later recorded by an up-and-coming singer named Frank Sinatra. Sinatra's recording of her song zoomed to the top, sold a huge number of records, and established him as a singer. Ruth Lowe had created something beautiful for herself and for the world.

The story of Ruth Lowe is unusual, of course. Had her husband lived, she might never have written that beautiful song and gone on to write many others. Who knows? Grief can be a powerful stimulator. But you don't have to have grief to create good songs. What sparks one mind to create songs may fall flat with another. Right now, whoever you are, whatever your age, and whatever your situation, you have the potential power to create new songs.

Ideas from Personal Experience

In remembering Ruth and her story, keep in mind at all times that your own personal experience may well yield some strong song ideas.

I wrote my first song from personal experience. While serving in the U.S. Navy, I was in New York City on two days' leave. I felt low that last afternoon in the city because my ship was leaving Boston the next day for an eight-month Mediterranean cruise.

While in the main library on 42nd Street, I read about a song contest being held by a music magazine. Rather than feel sorry for myself, I decided to spend my last afternoon in the States trying to write some words that might cheer up other people. By 5:30 that evening, I had finished a lyric to my liking and dropped it in the mail on the way back to my ship. I forgot all about the song, which I had called "There's Still Tomorrow."

Eight months later, home on leave, I read my published lyric in a national magazine. It had won first prize. After that, composers all over America wrote me, asking if they could write the music for my lyric. I finally agreed to let a New York composer do the music. While the song was never recorded, it was performed live in a number of nightclubs. Because of this first song, I got intensely interested in music and have been writing ever since. I've written hundreds of songs. A number of them have been published, recorded, or performed in various parts of the country. Two of them have won national awards.

Beyond the profit motivation for writing songs, it's a heck of a lot of fun. After seventeen years at it, I still love to create new songs and the pleasure I've had writing them has been enormous. Songwriting can bring you the same personal satisfaction. Then too, there's always the chance that you'll hit the jackpot with a song.

Keep Writing

A real songwriter—for pleasure or profit—is forever writing songs. As Irving Berlin once put it, "A true songwriter is alert for ideas while riding in a taxi, doing his daily job, or wherever he is." Keep writing them. Keep expressing yourself in words and/or music. Cole Porter was 38 before his success began in a big way, but he had been writing songs since he was a small boy. He had even had some shows on Broadway, but real success had eluded him. He never quit writing, and his musical ship finally came in with banners flying.

Always Carry a Notebook

Ideas for songs can come to you at any time, once you let your mind know you want them and stay on the alert for them. Be sure to have a notebook with you wherever you go, so you won't lose a possible good idea. Don't trust your memory. You may forget a good idea if you can't get it down for several hours.

When you are unsure about the worth of an idea, try the advice of Ted Mack: "Try to develop an awarenesss of the inner voice within your own heart." Be ever alert and even expectant for that big idea that is right for you. Experiment with your ideas, those that interest you and even the ones you feel unsure of, and see what happens. They might lead you to still better ideas.

Stay with ideas that interest you. The more you think about an idea, the more possibilities will come to your mind for that idea. Use the association method with your ideas. What is it related to? Let your mind wander. Play with an idea, nurse it along.

One excellent test for an idea is to try to put it out of your mind for several days. If it keeps popping into your mind, as if crying "don't forget me," then you probably have a good idea. Stick to it. Even those ideas that don't work out aren't necessarily losses. The work you put into them is bound to help you with other ideas. When you may least expect it, a topnotch idea may flash into your mind, almost like a sudden reward for your past work.

Other Sources of Song Ideas

You may also find ideas for new songs in the conversations of your family and friends, at movies, on television, in dreamland, at parties, meetings, or while traveling. Be ready for them when they come at any moment. You can always choose the best ones from your total list later.

2

Which to Do First—The Lyrics or Music?

Some say that this long-discussed question of which to do first—the lyrics or music—is like asking whether Santa Claus sleeps with his beard under the covers or on the outside. Keep in mind from the start that both the lyrics and music of a song are important. A fine lyric can be spoiled with the wrong kind of music and vice-versa. But sooner or later, you must decide whether you're going to write mostly lyrics, music, or both.

There are those in various phases of the music business who believe strongly that the lyrics are most important. Others will put up a good case for writing the music first.

After writing a number of songs, you'll be able to tell if you have the basic ability to do both music and lyrics. It's a great feeling to be in total control of the words and music. If you did the lyric yourself on a given song, you naturally know what kind of music you want for it. The same is true if you did the music.

On the other hand, it takes a very talented person to write both lyrics and music that are professional and/or commercial. Cole Porter did both of them well. Paul Anka does too. Kenny O'Dell, the writer of "Behind Closed Doors," is strong on both.

The advice of one of today's most successful writers, Paul Williams, is well worth thinking about: "Your chances for success as a songwriter will probably be much higher if you specialize in either words or music and get a collaborator to fill in on the other half."

Why Not Try Your Hand at Both?

There's certainly no harm in trying your hand at both lyrics and music. You're bound to find out which of the two you like best or feel most comfortable doing. And you'll soon learn which comes the easiest for you. You can also experiment by doing only the lyrics on some songs, or only the music on others, or both on still other ones. In fact, this is the quickest way to discover where your strength lies as a writer. If you're in songwriting for the long pull, you'll probably write a lot of songs before you're through. So you may prefer to do both the music and lyrics on at least some of your songs. After all, full royalties on a song are better than half any day.

Some Sound Reasons for Writing the Lyrics First

You can find major music publishers in Nashville, Hollywood, and New York who will tell you that they feel the lyrics are the most vital part of a song. Whether or not you agree with them you should consider some good reasons for actually writing the lyrics of your songs first.

There are 88 notes in music. This certainly gives you a wide choice of musical ideas to play around with. And it makes many think that coming up with a good new sound from so many note possibilities shouldn't be very difficult.

The point to remember is that this wide choice of music progression is always open to you with each new song you write. The fact that there are 88 notes encourages many writers to believe that a new tune can always be composed. To many songwriters, this is one good reason for doing the lyrics first.

Another excellent reason is because the lyric idea itself can sometimes suggest or inspire the right music. There's a sound, a rhythm, and a flow of the lyrics that can occasionally lead you to a good tune. But if the music is done first, you may find it harder to come up with words for the existing music line.

I got the lyric idea for one of my own songs while wandering around a Civil War battlefield one day. Before I finished the lyrics a few weeks later, I began to get music ideas. The lyric I had been thinking about and working on inspired the music. I read the words out loud (this always helps) until various musical phrases came to mind. I then worked out the music I wanted on both piano and guitar. If you like the lyrics on a given song and feel they're what you want to say, good musical ideas may not be far behind.

Are Your Musical Ideas Truly Original?

A word of warning is in order here. It's a good rule to be suspicious at first of music ideas that come to you. The human mind is strange. It can sometimes present a writer with what you might first think is an original musical phrase or idea. But that great melody you think is yours can easily turn out to be someone else's work.

All of us hear music everywhere these days—in stores, offices, elevators, as well as on records, radio, and television. This adds up to a lot of music floating around inside our heads. So when you're trying to compose a new sound, remember that your mind can trick you if you aren't careful. Let those new tunes that come to you simmer for a few days. Or let someone else hear your music. Make sure the music you compose is really new and original.

It's true of course that parts of different songs do sound alike or remind us of other songs. But a good general rule to follow is to be suspicious if more than four or five straight measures of your music are exactly like any other song tune. Try to keep the music of your songs fresh and different. A few measures now and then are bound to be similar to other songs, but don't let it get out of hand. With 88 notes to work with, new music sounds shouldn't be a problem.

More Reasons for Writing the Lyrics First

There are other reasons for writing the lyrics first. Lyric ideas are usually easier to get down on paper. Most serious songwriters carry a notebook with them at all times. But capturing an idea for new music is often more difficult. You may not be near a guitar or piano. Unless you find it easy to remember a new musical phrase—and not forget it until you can get to a guitar or piano—you may lose some good music ideas. This has happened to many songwriters; they've lost musical ideas as well as lyrics because of not getting them down on paper.

Don't trust your memory. Wherever you go, have paper and pen with you. One writer I know always keeps 3 x 5 note cards in his pockets. As most songwriters will admit, some of the best ideas come at odd times. One of my own best song ideas hit me while I was riding on a crowded subway in New York City. I fortunately had a notebook with me. Hoagy Carmichael got the idea for "Stardust" while walking across the campus of his alma mater, Indiana University, one night.

Richard Hadden is an ASCAP writer, composer, and pianist. He and his wife, Frances, have worked on many musical shows, including several that were on Broadway. Hadden has long believed that the lyrics determine a great deal about a song: "This is why I seldom sit down and simply make up a melody. A song says something, otherwise it is not a song. So, in my opinion, the idea should come first. Oscar Hammerstein, in his early collaborations, always wrote his words to tunes, because that was the way he worked in those days. Later, with Rodgers, he wrote the lyrics first."

Starting with the music first for a new song may also possibly lead you into problems in fitting those words to the already existing music. You might, for example, be forced to cut certain words from the lyrics or have to change several lines. And such forced changes could possibly alter the meaning and overall effect of your song, thus hurting its success.

Another plus for writing the lyrics first is the title of your song. A strong and attractive title might well lead you eventually to a complete lyric, as well as to the key musical phrase or melodic idea for your song. Titles can sometimes do this. They can stimulate you so much that you get fired up and turn out a strong or highly commercial complete song.

A final reason for doing the lyrics first is for the plain fun of it. A great many songwriters just enjoy writing the lyrics before even thinking about the music. The challenge for these writers lies mostly in the lyrics—the story, the mood, and what they want the song to say.

If you write many songs, you will discover that sometimes there is no set way to write certain songs. Songwriting is an art. Some songs just won't be forced into creation any certain way. You may do the lyrics first on most of the songs that you write. The music will come to you first on the other songs. And on those marvelous days when your creative songwriting juices are really flowing, you'll get both the words and music at the same time or very close to each other. Days like these are bonuses and can possibly bring you a smash hit song. Be ready for such days when they come.

Despite the reasons we've given for writing the lyrics first, if a good music idea haunts you, by all means get it down on paper or on tape. You can always try for the lyrics later. In other words, be receptive to new music ideas, even though you write the lyrics first most of the time. Who knows? You might wake up some morning humming a hit tune. It can happen. But I think you'll find that most of the time it's wiser to write the lyrics first and then go from there.

3

Writing the Words of Your Song

By now you're no doubt aware that the words of a song are also often referred to as either the lyrics or the lyric idea. No matter which term you use, you're dealing with the story, mood, emotion, or feeling of your song. The words or lyrics must sing and get through to the listener.

Writer and artist Ray Stevens believes that a song must be relevant. "Songwriting is storytelling in capsulized form. It's not hard to rhyme. The problem is saying something relevant—something that touches people, gets inside the listener, penetrates to what turns the listener on."

To write the most commercial lyrics possible, you need to give some thought to when and where you can do your best writing. this will take some time to discover, but it can be a great help to you.

Take television's Michael Landon as an example. Though he's not a songwriter, Landon is an excellent television script writer. Part of his secret is the fact that he's found out how and where he does his best writing.

Landon has always written in longhand. He likes to sit on the floor in front of a coffee table to do his writing. "When you are affluent, you have an office to write in . . . and when the super-decorator got through with my super office, putting in a super-desk, I found I could not write at all. My brain goes dead when I try to write at a desk, so I had to bring in a coffee table and sit on the floor again."

You must do the same, that is, find out what conditions work best for you in your songwriting. If you do your best writing at 2 A.M., go to it at that early hour. Whatever works best for you is the routine to stick with.

Sources for New Song Lyrics

Chapter 1 explained that new song ideas are all around you at all times. The following list includes some additional good sources. Lyric ideas may come from:

1. Other songs you hear. A line, even a word, may suggest a new idea to you.

2. Your own life, both past and present—even your future. Search your memory for things that have happened to you, along with your daily routine. Dream of what may happen.

3. Short and long travel. Even a brief weekend trip to the country can bring new lyric ideas.

4. Conversations you may hear on buses, trains, planes, or in stores, at camp, conferences, at school or college, at business meetings, luncheons, parties, weddings, conventions, and just about everywhere.

5. The experiences and emotions of others revealed and communicated in films, books, and television.

6. Your own emotions. Every time you feel sad, blue, happy, angry, disappointed, keep your mind open for possible lyric ideas. Remember. Millions of others have felt the same way.

7. All kinds of newspapers and magazines are gold mines of new lyric ideas.

8. Special feature columns that give readers advice on their emotional problems offer a continuing source of potential lyric ideas.

The above list is by no means a complete one. But it gives the key sources where many strong lyric ideas have originated.

An excellent way to keep yourself always alert for new lyric ideas is to keep a master file or special record book of new lyric ideas, song titles, or lyric fragments. You cannot count on getting much of the lyric at first. All you may think of from your original inspiration may be just a title, the first line, a last line, or merely a word or two. From whatever you start out with, you then have to build, shape, and develop a professional lyric.

The act or practice of writing down every possible lyric idea you think might be developed into an effective song will stimulate your mind to be constantly on the lookout for new ideas. Well-known writers use this very method. In other words, a pocket notebook (or index cards) can be used to put down your ideas as you go about your daily routine. You should write down anything you feel has potential, whether it's just a few words or several lines.

You can later transfer all the ideas that you think have potential from your daily notebook to your master file.

This collecting of lyrics, lyric ideas, or fragments can become a way of life. If you stick to it, you'll have a continually growing file of new lyric ideas. You may not use all of them or even write complete songs on half of them. But having your own master file of potential lyric ideas will give you a confident feeling, like a squirrel who knows he's put away a good supply of nuts for the winter.

On those days when you're trying hard to write a good

lyric, you can easily check over the ideas in your special file. You may find just the idea you want to work on or develop. Something in your file may help you over a rough spot in a lyric you already have underway. Some top professional writers jot down key words and phrases on scraps of paper and throw them all into a box or carton at the end of a day or a week. A lot of hit songs have gotten started this very way.

How to Start a Song Lyric

Many songwriters have their own methods of beginning a new lyric, but here are some suggestions that often work well:

1. Start a lyric from a feeling. Some examples are "King of the Road," "Jealousy," "I'm So Lonesome I Could Cry." There are many human feelings that can lead you into some very commercial lyrics. There's even a song called "Feelings" that's performed time and again. This hit song hits people hard; they identify with the lyric.

2. Start a lyric from a word or phrase. Some examples of this method are "It's Wonderful," "Heartaches by the Numbers," and "You and Me Against the World." When you think about the number of words, phrases, and lines that can pass through the mind of an alert songwriter in a given day, you get a good idea of why a songwriter must learn to screen the gems from the pebbles.

Kenny O'Dell, hit writer of "Behind Closed Doors" and other top chart numbers, gets many of his songs from a little phrase or a slang word that people say: "Ideas sometimes jump out at me and demand I write them. It's frustrating. One day you are grumbling if you can't get one line, then it all comes out, you hear it in the studio, and it sounds pretty good."

3. Start a lyric from an object. Some examples are "Love

Letters in the Sand," "Lipstick on My Collar," and "Blue Suede Shoes." Speaking of "Suedes," it was the first song ever to be in top place in the country, rhythm and blues, and pop charts, at the same time. It was a big hit for Carl Perkins, and for Elvis Presley too. Perkins was appearing at a dance one night, so the story goes, when he saw a girl accidentally smudge her dancing partner's shoe. Perkins heard the boy say:"Hey, don't step on my suedes." From that spark of a great idea, Perkins worked on it and developed it into a hit.

4. Start a lyric from a person's name. "Jean" has done all right for Rod McKuen. Remember "Big Bad John"? It was a huge hit for country singer Jimmy Dean, who also wrote it. "Ode to Billy Joe" even led to a movie based on the song. This method alone can lead you to countless lyric ideas and eventually complete songs.

When you listen to songs, do some thinking about what the source of the lyric may have been. This practice can help you in writing your own lyrics.

5. Start a lyric from a place or name of a city: "By the Time I Get to Phoenix," "Rose Garden," and "I Left My Heart in San Francisco" have all made fortunes. City songs can become enormous hits and often appeal to all kinds of music lovers.

6. Start a lyric from an image or word-created picture. Some examples here are "Cry," "On the Street Where You Live," "Slow Boat to China," and "The Green Green Grass of Home." Such songs create pictures in the listener's mind that are easily remembered. The appeal to the senses can be used effectively in song lyrics.

7. Start a lyric from a question. "What Kind of Fool Am I?" became a click standard that asked this same question over and over. Other examples are "Do You Feel Like We Do?" and "How Deep Is the Ocean?"

8. Start a lyric with words that deal with time in some

way. Some examples for this type are "Yesterday," "The Last Time I Saw Paris," "Always," and "I Could Have Danced All Night."

9. Start a lyric from words that sound like a virtual command. Examples include "Fool Me," "Take Good Care of My Baby," "Put Your Head on My Shoulder," "Make the World Go Away," and "Release Me." When you hear various songs, try to listen for these command title numbers. They are usually strong lyrics. An evaluation of the hot 100-chart songs in the nation during any given week will just about always reveal a healthy number of such command-type songs.

10. Start a lyric with a statement. The top song charts are usually well represented with this type of lyric. Examples include "I'm Easy," "You're the Best Thing That Ever Happened to Me," "I Never Had It So Good," and "I Won't Last a Day Without You."

There are still other ways to begin a lyric, but using the above ten methods will give you some good practice and stimulate your thinking about lyrics in general.

Lyrics Are a Challenge

Writing song lyrics is a challenge. It gets in your blood after awhile and can stay with you for life. Many who write lyrics, whether they're well-known writers or not, are filled with the fascination of working with words and ideas.

If you want to see one or more of your songs riding high on the charts some day, or if you wish to keep your name in the ranks of successful writers (in case you're already a proven professional), then you've got to think about song ideas and lyrics wherever you go and whatever you may be doing. Some fortunate writers can turn their lyric writing ability on and off like water, but most writers have to mine for the gold. And that means doing some hard thinking.

Just try to stay mentally alert, so you won't miss any good lyric ideas.

I once got a lyric idea, while merely driving on a Tennessee highway in the rain. I noticed that the highway had one dangerous curve after another. When I stopped for gas in a small town, I talked to an old-timer who was having a Coke at the station. He told me that the highway was considered one of the most dangerous in the nation. Many people have lost their lives on its various curves.

Before I hit the Virginia state line, a lyric had started forming in my mind. It turned out to be a story lyric about a driver who has an ESP experience on a strange highway in Tennessee. Here are several lines:

> There's a road in Tennessee
> Not fit for man or beast
> The highway where the vultures
> Have a human bloody feast
> Knoxville lay behind me, Kingsport miles ahead
> And through the rain the devil's voice
> "Two curves and you'll be dead
> Two curves and you'll be dead."

I think that most writers try to do lyrics about lost love, jilted romance, cheating lovers, and the realities of life. At least these are some very commercial topics. But other types of lyrics will sometimes demand to be written. They may never become complete songs, and if they do, they may never be recorded. But they still have to be written— by writers who can't get them out of their minds except by writing them.

In other words, you may have to write a lot of lyrics before things can start moving in your songwriting. So keep in mind that the work you do on many lyrics that don't ever become complete songs is helping to lead you to those four-star lyrics and songs that can make it all the way. A songwriter is a person who writes—whether it's lyrics, music, or both. You write. And you keep writing, whether you have three songs recorded or 300—one hit, twenty hits, or no hits at all. You write because you're a songwriter. It's as simple as that.

In the course of your writing career, you'll probably write all types of songs, unless you decide to focus on a special kind of song. Some of your lyrics will naturally be more commercial than others. The song idea I got on a Tennessee highway is just one example that lyric ideas can come to you at anytime.

Try to Write Lyrics That Are Timeless

The large majority of the songs I've written have been ballads. It always seemed to me that many of the biggest songs of any year are ballads. They seem to be timeless. I still feel this way. But I've written every kind of song in the book. And you probably will too.

Back in the early 1970s, the film *Patton* created quite a stir. I thought at the time that a song about Patton might be right as either an album number or as a single. I couldn't get the idea out of my mind. I finally worked out a lyric I called "The Ballad of George Patton." One of my collaborators at the time, John Sanicola, did the music. The song came together. And it was no drag. It moved. A respected music publisher in Nashville accepted our demo and thought enough of the song to try to interest some record labels. As it turned out, the song was never recorded. But it came close, and I'm still glad I wrote it. Here are some lines from the lyric:

> From California to West Point
> He followed his own star
> To beat the German desert fox

In the bloody game of war
He cursed like a stable boy
But prayed on his knees
That was George Patton
Man of destiny.

At least one publisher agreed that there was a market for this type of song. Songwriter Don Wayne wrote one called "MacArthur's Hand" in 1971. The song was published by Tree Music and recorded by Cal Smith.

Try to learn from your songs that don't make it. If a lyric is not timeless, the resulting song can be hurt. My Patton song had limited appeal because it lacked this important quality of being timeless. But I wrote it thinking it might be right for an album. And who knows? It might have added to any number of record albums of the early 1970s.

A Hit Song Can Be Elusive

A hit song is an elusive thing. You have to do your best on many songs and hope for some occasional quality mixed in with the quantity. The lyrics you create are going to be right on the target, very close, fairly close, or out there somewhere in left field. But don't worry about it—just do your best and go on to the next song. Write a lot of songs and give the law of averages a chance to work for you.

But do try for this timeless quality. "Stardust" is a timeless song. The same is true of "Release Me," "Danny Boy," "All the Way," "Yesterday" (by the Beatles), and a hundred others that come to mind. There's no doubt about it. The songs that stick around to become standards are timeless songs.

Lyric Construction Patterns

For many years, a lyric wasn't really considered a song

lyric if it didn't conform to one of the basic lyric construction patterns (usually **AABA**, **ABAB**, **ABAC**, and verse-chorus). This is certainly no longer true for the pop music field. The writing style is freer today, and not bound by any set pattern. A number of songs in the country field still use the basic verse-chorus-verse-chorus construction. "Country Roads" is a good example.

So you have much more freedom today as a songwriter in just about all music areas. But use the traditional lyric patterns, if you wish. Many fine songs are still written around them. It's up to you. You're the writer.

The Importance of Simplicity

The first thing you should do when you finish a new lyric is to put it through a simplicity test. If every line in your lyric isn't immediately understandable, cross it out and rewrite it. A song lyric is meant to be sung. So it must be simple.

Here's one way you can prove to yourself that simple lyrics are vital to successful songwriting. Listen to the records being played on the radio and write down the titles of the songs you hear with simple lyrics. You'll have a lot of them listed in no time at all. The same is true with the top-selling records in the stores. Most of them are songs with simple lyrics.

The sound of the lines of a lyric can have a real impact on listeners. But to accomplish this they have got to be simple. How do you keep a lyric simple? Don't make it too long; don't go off on some other angle in the middle of your lyric; stick with the theme or premise of your lyric.

There's a Difference Between Lyrics and Poetry

Never think of yourself as a poet. You're not writing poetry; you're writing words and lines to be performed, hopefully by name recording artists. Strive to write lyrics that are easily sung. Here are some proven ways to focus on the difference between lyrics and poetry:

1. Find the stuffiest poem you can and then try to sing it out loud.
2. Sing the lyrics out loud of "Rudolph the Red-Nosed Reindeer." These lyrics are saturated with four-star simplicity.
3. Read the song lyric magazines regularly. You'll find them on sale at most newsstands. These lyrics are from songs that are being recorded and sold in the stores. Study the lyrics in each issue. You might even rewrite them or try to improve them if you can. Try to determine what the strong points are of each lyric.

Keep Your Lyrics Clean

I know you're aware that the subject matter of today's songs is much wider. Many song lyrics are suggestive. Some say it's just a cycle we're going through that will end.

Try not to confuse honesty with suggestiveness. A lyric can have an impact without being suggestive or dirty. You want your songs to appeal to as many as possible, so stick with clean lyrics. You'll be better off in the long run. Most of the songs that get recorded and performed many times through the years have clean lyrics.

Bringing a Lyric to Life

For the sake of illustration, I want to explain how I wrote a lyric from a title that I just couldn't forget. This example will show you how a lyric can be created from an idea or title alone. I've forgotten where I got the title idea, but it kept pestering me to be written. So I went ahead and started it. The title was "Dress Rehearsal for the Blues."

I let the title kick around in my cluttered songwriter's

brain for a few weeks. Then I sat down one night after dinner and came up with four lines. The singer of the song is telling the one leaving him (or her) that he needs time to get used to the idea of their splitting up. This produced the following lines:

> Before you walk away and leave me cryin'
> I need some help in learnin' how to lose
> I need time to get used to your leavin'
> I need a "DRESS REHEARSAL FOR THE BLUES"

I next reasoned that the second stanza would state the same idea but in a slightly different way. The second section of lines in many lyrics often does just this. Here are the next lines I wrote:

> Re-living your goodbye will be my madness
> Like rubbing shoulders with a lighted fuse
> For you can't snuggle up to a mem'ry
> Without a DRESS REHEARSAL FOR THE BLUES.

The bridge of a song today is defined by some in different ways. Some songs don't even have one. If the lyric construction pattern fits, I still believe it often helps to have a bridge. The total effect of many songs with bridges is strengthened. Some lyrics don't produce bridges, and it's also true that some writers are confused as to what a bridge is supposed to be.

The bridge is basically meant to offer relief from the main melody line, and also from the central theme of the lyric. The words of the bridge (often a stanza) approach the song subject from a fresh viewpoint, before returning again to the theme. The same is true of the music. The bridge music is different from the major melodic line. If your lyric falls in the ABBA pattern of construction, it means that the B-part is the bridge. Remember, many of the greatest songs ever written have bridges and have, in fact, used the ABBA construction pattern. My bridge lines for the lyric came out as follows:

> Funny thing about life
> The old cliches are true
> I ignored the one I loved
> And now I'm lonely too.

The last section of a lyric often reinforces the theme and ends with the title used again and/or with an extra bit of flash or punch. My last four lines came out this way:

> So once you hit the big leagues with a true love
> Don't pull out all the stops, pick up your clues
> So your pride takes a walk, what about it
> It beats a DRESS REHEARSAL FOR THE BLUES
> It beats a DRESS REHEARSAL FOR THE BLUES.

You can see from this illustration that a lyric can often be written from a title that you like or can't forget. As it turned out, I never came up with any music for the above lyric that I liked well enough, so it's still just half a song. This happens to songwriters. Sometimes you can't get the right music for certain lyrics and vice-versa.

You will notice that I managed to get the title into the lyric four times. Try to do this whenever you can in your own lyrics. You want the song to be remembered and that means the title preferably must stick in the listener's mind.

Steve Allen, a successful songwriter himself, heard about the above song and praised it; perhaps that's reason enough for the writing of "Dress Rehearsal for the Blues." You might like to try your own talents at writing a lyric to this title. If so, be my guest. You can't copyright a title, so you're welcome to write your own lyric version of this song title. And good luck.

You Learn by Writing Lots of Lyrics

You can write lyrics about practically everything. But naturally some of the resulting lyrics won't be as commercial as others. I still think a lyricist should write a lot, acting on the premise that some of his or her lyrics are going to be very commercial. The others can either be rewritten or filed away as deadwood.

Al Dubin, one of the great songwriters of the past, averaged 60 songs a year for 15 years. And many of the resulting songs were hits.

Dubin also supports the view that observation can be of help in lyric writing. He worked out his own formula for creating song hits, and it's well worth highlighting here: "Usually, I try to express the ideas of young people. For example, I'm sitting one night in the Coconut Grove on the west coast. It was at the depth of the depression and all around me are beautiful young dames dancing with middle-aged men. And these dames aren't smiling. So I started to ask myself, "What are they saying to themselves in their hearts?" I finally came up with the answer: 'Dancing with Tears in My Eyes.' I must have been right, too." He was right. The song was a smash hit.

So hang in there with your lyric writing. Keep at it, and I predict that you'll make your mark in songwriting.

4

Rewriting Can Improve Your Lyric

You've no doubt heard the saying that "big money songs aren't written; they're rewritten into hits." Well, many of them are. For every writer who claims that he or she dashes off a hit lyric in fifteen or thirty minutes, there are probably a hundred others doing rewrites on their lyrics to give them a fighting chance to compete.

How much rewriting is needed? It depends on the songwriter and the particular song in question. A writer like Hal David or Paul Williams may not have to do nearly as much rewriting as the average songwriter. Years of writing experience naturally help a lot.

Ace lyricist Hal David feels that writers shouldn't fall in love too quickly with the lyrics they do. You've got to be objective about the lines you write even if it means putting the lyric away and forgetting it for several days. You'll come back to it with a fresh viewpoint. Roger Miller, one of the best songwriters in the country, claims that he wrote his hit "Dang Me" in five minutes, but admits "King of the Road" took longer. Miller has been called a natural songwriter. He turns out new songs continually and evidently with little effort. And he can write them anywhere.

But for the large majority of songwriters, getting a strong and commercial lyric that really says something, and says it well, means polishing the lines again and again. To make real money with your songs, try to resist the temptation to be too easily satisfied with what you write. Ask yourself over and over how you can improve each lyric. Many well-known writers do considerable rewriting, despite the stories you hear about hit songs being created in twenty minutes. The days on which hits come quickly are rewards for all the previous days of rewriting and polishing other songs.

The Art of Rewriting

Rewriting your lyrics can become an art in itself. It can be some of the most valuable time spent on your song. What good is a highly commercial tune or music sound that fits your lyric perfectly, if the lyric itself is fuzzy, confusing, or weak? Rewriting the lyric until you're convinced that it's absolutely the best you can do is one sure way to turn out more attractive songs. Only after you've given your all on the entire lyric are you ready to proceed further with the song.

If polishing up a lyric comes hard for you, just remember that a hit song can be a cash bonanza. But realize, too, that it's tougher today to come up with huge hits. More people than ever are trying to write hit songs. But more competition doesn't mean that you can't become a successful and prosperous songwriter one day. A song doesn't have to be an enormous hit to make money. the mini-hits do well, too.

Rewriting will add strength to your song lyrics and

make them stand out over competing songs. Part of the art of rewriting is psychological. Convince yourself of the value of rewriting, and then put it into practice.

One good way to rewrite a lyric is to take each line separately and check it out for clarity. Is it simple? Could anyone hearing it understand it at once? Are the words in the line too long with too many syllables? It's far better to stick with words of one or two syllables. Do the first several lines of the lyric convey the story, mood, or emotion of the song and hold the listener's attention? Is there some conflict in your lyric or lyric story? What use have you made of alliteration (the use of two or more words in sequence that start with the same letter)? It improves lines and makes them sing.

Rewriting may also take the form of redoing your lyric's rhyme scheme to make the rhymes more natural and effective. Many songs get away with false rhymes today, but it's more professional to use true rhymes. The words "time" and "mine," for example, do not truly rhyme. They only sound similar. Watch and listen for false rhymes in the songs you hear. There are plenty of them around. You may sometimes have to work harder and longer to get a true rhyme and you may have to change the words a number of times, but it makes for a more attractive lyric.

Sometimes, an inner rhyme can help a lyric line. This is a word often in the middle of a line that rhymes with another word and/or possibly with the word at the end of that same line. Don't overdo the rhymes in your lyrics, but do use them as effectively as you can. Finding a good rhyme scheme for their lyrics is part of the fun and challenge of songwriting for many writers.

Whenever you have to rewrite a lyric, keep in mind that this is one of the necessary writing disciplines that can one day bring you success. Oscar Hammerstein was a brilliant lyricist, but he wasn't above changing a line and polishing

it up over and over until he got what he wanted. He sometimes worked for weeks and longer to get a line or phrase
the way he desired. As a result, his songs are unforgettable.

"I give him a lyric and get out of his way, Hammerstein
once said of his partnership with Richard Rodgers. To call
Hammerstein's words of haunting beauty and deep wis-
dom just lyrics seems inadequate. His lyrics are gems, romantic jewels of starlight that go straight to the listener's
heart. He communicated.

Hammerstein was basically a romantic optimist who believed completely in love's lasting magic. He lifted high
that magic through his simple but appealing lyrics. As he
often admitted: "I just can't write anything without hope
in it." Almost 1,000 lyrics flowed from this genius with
words, including such all-time great numbers as "Some
Enchanted Evening," "The Last Time I Saw Paris," all
the songs from "South Pacific," "Oklahoma," and "The
Sound of Music."

Study the lyrics left behind by Hammerstein and the
positive philosophy of the man will come across to you.
He believed that one must face his or her problems and
overcome them. He clearly believed that good wins over
evil. He saw the bad and the tragic in the world but responded to the urge to "keep saying there are beautiful
meadows bathed in sunshine." He felt such things should
be said, too, "because they're just as true."

What does this mean to you? Simply that if you write
enough lyrics and songs, something of yourself, your style,
your beliefs, your basic feelings about life in general may
be revealed. Hammerstein of course wrote mostly for
Broadway musicals in which songs are especially created
to fit certain plot situations.

Hammerstein was a hard worker. He sometimes spent
from three to six weeks on a simple lyric. He liked to stand
while working on a lyric. He had a good reason for rewrit-

ing, polishing and striving for just the right   words: he wanted every song and every show to be a real success.

If show tunes interest you, spend some time reading and studying the deceptively simple and delightful lyrics of Oscar Hammerstein. Even though the type of Broadway musical he wrote for has changed, a study of his lyrics will give you a good foundation for show tune lyrics.

How to Make a New Lyric Start

Whenever a lyric just won't work out right no matter how much you try, you might just start all over. Try to think of whatever the lyric may be about from another angle. At such times when you feel bogged down with a lyric, try writing the last part of the lyric. Then work toward the ending you have. This method often works well in finishing troublesome lyrics.

Rewriting Is Really Persistence

This whole business of rewriting is another way of saying that you've got to be persistent in your efforts to write lyrics that will click commercially. Vincent Van Gogh didn't create his magnificent paintings overnight. The Mona Lisa wasn't dashed off in a week. Cole Porter would often be on a troublesome lyric mentally while physically attending a boring dinner party.

Try hard to make the lyrics you write sparkle. Make them snap, crackle, and beg for an appropriate musical accompaniment. Make them so strong and attractive that record labels, publishers, and artists will be eager to use them. And then you'll be glad you spent that time and effort rewriting.

5

Setting Your Lyrics to Music

Once you have a lyric to your liking, the next step is to get appropriate music. Don't waste your time trying to interest a market in just a lyric alone. You need complete songs to market, whether you write both the lyrics and music yourself or collaborate with another writer.

How to Get Melody Ideas

One of the best and most common ways to get a melody idea is from the lyrics you have already written. Simply read over the lyrics until you begin to get a feeling for the rhythm (the rise and fall) of the lines. Some writers tap out the beats and rhythm of a lyric with a pen or pencil. Before doing this, it will help you to go through the entire lyric and place accent marks over the word syllables that are stressed (where the beat falls). Here is an example:

> The world is young no more.

You can see that the beat or stress falls on the words *world, young*, and *more*. These words are stressed naturally when the line is read out loud.

After you place the beat (or stress) marks on each line of your lyric, you should be able to tap out the rhythm of your lyric. Keep at it and think about the rhythm your lyric seems to suggest. Melodic ideas will come to you if you have even a basic feeling for music.

The words and the lines, together with where the beat falls, often suggest a tune. You may have to experiment, but tunes can be written this way. The stressed word syllables of your lyric usually, but not always, mean that the notes for those syllables will be of a longer value.

Another obvious way to compose a melody is to sit down at the piano or with a guitar and try your ideas to see if they sound interesting. Take the opening line of the chorus of your lyric, or the very first opening line, and try for a key melodic phrase (several measures of music that express the main theme of your music). A good example of a melodic phrase is the melody of the first two lines of "Carry Me Back to Old Virginia."

Once you have a good melodic phrase that seems to fit the opening lines of your lyric (or the chorus), you have the central musical idea for your entire lyric. This same melodic phrase can be repeated with slight variations. You may have half of your job finished, once you compose a key melodic phrase.

If you're doing the music first (and don't yet have a lyric), you have more freedom in creating a melody phrase. Simply try to devise an appealing phrase that will cover several measures. Then try later to fit one or two lines of your lyric to the existing melody.

Another tool in writing melodies is the term "motive." A motive is just a short melody idea consisting of no more than four notes. An example of a motive is the melody for "how dry I am." The four notes that represent that phrase musically is a motive.

Therefore, the two types of melodic ideas are a phrase (a melodic phrase that covers a line or two of lyrics) and a motive (a short melody fragment of four notes). An understanding of both motives and phrases can be of help to you when composing new music.

It's very possible that you may get a melody idea at the same time you get the lyric or title idea. Look over the titles of many songs from the past and you'll realize that the key musical idea is contained in the title line or the line leading up to the title line. Examples are "Always" and "Blue Skies."

Keep in mind that when you originate a new song title you may also have a melody to fit the title. Try to play that title on the piano or guitar, making up the music to fit it. "If Ever I Would Leave You" is a perfect example. The main kernel of the melody is the title line. That main melody keeps repeating throughout the song with variations.

How to Write the Basic Tune Down

You don't have to be able to write a lead sheet, but it will help you in your songwriting if you can learn to do it. A lead sheet is simply the musical notation on sheet music of a song. It has the main melodic line (the notes) of the song with each word or word syllable of the lyric below each corresponding note. The chord progressions or changes are also indicated above the measures throughout the song.

Once you have composed even a complete one-finger melody line of your song, write down the notes and simply add the words of your lyric below the matching notes. If you don't understand the basic notes and their values, a short period of study will clear up any confusion. If you can play tunes on the piano with one finger, you should be able to write a lead sheet. Just learn how the notes of the scale (quarter-notes, half-notes, whole-notes, eighth-notes, and dotted notes) are written down on paper. Then some-

one else can whip it into shape for you or check on the
accuracy.

Never send an incorrect lead sheet of your song to a
market. Make sure that it's right. Then have copies made.
A crude lead sheet is okay, however, when you're experimenting and working out your new tunes for yourself.

I still personally believe that the lyrics come first in the
majority of songs. Music ideas, however, may come to you
at times. And you may never get lyrics for them. What you
might have in this event is an instrumental piece, a musical number without words. All you need then is a title for
the instrumental. Irving Berlin wrote "Alexander's Ragtime Band" without words. He added the lyrics later. The
song made him rich and famous at the ripe old age of 23.

How to Compose Melodies Without Touching a Piano or Guitar

If you don't play piano or guitar, you can still compose.
You can hum, can't you? As long as you can hum your
melody idea, you can be a composer. Hum your original
tune (or sing the words of your lyric) on tape. Then you
can pay a small fee to a local musician, music teacher, or
arranger to do a professional lead sheet for you from your
tape. The trade publications advertise various firms that
will transcribe your tune or complete song for a fee. The
idea is to get the melody line of your song down on paper.

Composing on the Piano or Guitar

If you have any feeling for music (even though you cannot
play well at all), you may find with a little experimenting
on the piano or guitar that you can get music ideas from
just playing a few basic chords. It's not difficult to learn
the basic chords for the piano or guitar used most often in
songwriting. Once you know them, you might get new
tune ideas by just playing a series of different chord

changes. If you have a good ear for music, you may find this is a stimulating way to compose.

With a phrase or line of lyrics in front of you, trying out different chords may lead you to some music ideas you can use.

What Kind of Melodies to Use

The title and style of the lyrics will usually determine what kind of melody or music your song needs. Keep in mind that there are all kinds of melodies. If you're writing for the teen market, then your melody should be oriented towards the kind of music teenagers like to buy. They often care more about the beat than the quality of the music itself.

Since the early 1970s, there has been a trend toward a softer pattern of melody and lyric forms. Some song examples of this trend include "Close to You" and the Perry Como hit, "It's Impossible."

The best way to keep up with the changing trends in music is to watch the trade publications closely. They accurately report on any new trends that may be developing or that seem to be having an influence in the industry. You can then compose your music with such helpful information in mind.

Composing the Right Music for Your Lyrics

Nothing can ruin your song like having the wrong music for the type of lyrics you've written. Assuming you have a lyric you want to compose music for, here are some pointers that will help you to create the right music:

1. Think about the title of the song and the overall feeling conveyed in the lyrics. Is it a happy song? Or is it sad? Is it soft rock, patriotic, religious, blues, country and western, a sophisticated show tune, or a big ballad? I once

wrote a lyric I called "Make Like an Atom and Split." It was a teen expression I had heard somewhere. The title itself clearly revealed that it was a teenage song. One of my collaborators did some very appropriate music for my lyric, and we had a song with strong teen appeal.

2. Compare your song lyrics with current songs on the market. If it seems to be similar in style to some other songs already out, then you might use a similar type of music.

3. If you're still unable to decide what kind of music is best for your lyrics, set the words aside for a few days. When you come back to your lyrics, you may have a fresh idea for the music.

4. Never forget that the songs you compose are written to be played, sung, and listened to. In order to please publishers, artists, and the key A & R people that produce songs, the song must not be too difficult.

5. Be careful not to match a contemporary lyric with outdated music or vice versa. To be suitable for a number of song markets, both the lyrics and music have to blend well. This used to be referred to as a perfect wedding between the words and music. Many publishers still think it's very important, regardless of what type of song it may be.

6. There's one exception to number five. If your song is written-composed especially for one of today's musical groups, the most important thing about your song will be the sound. The lyrics and music will be important but the right beat will be predominant.

7. Watch the range of your music. Too many songwriters forget that the voice range of the average singer is limited to about ten notes.

8. Don't let your music run too long. To compete today, a song should preferably be less than 3½ minutes. Anything beyond this may not be played by radio station disc jockeys. They have to get a lot of commercials into every

time segment. The length of your lyrics will often give you a good idea of about how long the music will run. Too many stanzas of lyrics or musical interludes will take extra time. "MacArthur Park" was a very long number, and it did well. But long numbers are rarely heard on radio.

9. Do your utmost to compose a melody that will be remembered. This is a must for a hit song.

A Final Word

If you feel inadequate to write music, don't let it keep you out of songwriting. You can definitely learn enough to get your own music either down on paper or onto a tape recorder. To get it in formal or professional shape (a lead sheet), you can pay a fee. You can also line up several composer collaborators to cowrite with you. Then you can virtually forget about the music, except for making suggestions to your collaborators as to the type of music you feel your lyrics need.

On the other hand, it's very true that lyricists often have a good basic feel for music. And composers often have a better-than-average understanding of lyrics. You and your cowriters might be more successful, if each of you (each of your collaborators along with yourself) knows something about each other's part of the song.

If you love music strongly, you should specialize in writing it. Broadway composer and lyricist Stephen Sondheim does both music and lyrics well. But he has discovered through experience that "music is always easier for me to write because it has to do with emotional atmosphere. I love music with a passion and always have." In other words, although he can do very effective lyrics, he prefers to do the music.

Try to compose some every day. Keep what you feel is successful and forget the rest. Nobody creates a hit tune every time he or she sits down. Keep at it. You'll write your share of worthwhile music.

6

Collaboration: Finding a Composer for Your Words or a Lyricist for Your Music

If you write only the lyrics or the music for songs, collaboration is a must. The music industry feeds on complete songs. Half a song is of little use to anyone . . . to you, a publisher, record company, or recording artist.

Collaboration has opened the doors for many writers. Songwriting teams have been some of the most successful writers in the business: Hal David and Burt Bacharach; Rodgers and Hammerstein; Lerner and Lowe; Sammy Cahn and Jimmy Van Heusen; Jerry Foster and Bill Rice; Ira and George Gershwin; and Henry Mancini and Johnny Mercer.

Unless you feel very strongly that you can write complete songs that are commercial enough to compete with all the others in today's song market, you should consider collaboration. That means finding a capable composer to do the music for your lyrics, or a capable lyricist to write the words for your music. Once you have a complete song, you have a product you can market and promote.

There are plenty of music-for-a-fee companies in the nation that will praise your work and supply the other half of your song. Beware of such firms. Nine times out of ten, the music you get for your lyrics, or the lyrics for your music, will be of a poor quality. Especially try to avoid replying to the classified ads you often see in numerous magazines offering to set your words to music for a price. Ads in the major music publications, however, are usually okay.

The right kind of collaboration is what you need. You want a composer who knows music well enough to give your lyrics a professional sounding musical setting. The same goes for finding a lyricist who can come up with a commercial lyric for your music. Many known and unknown writers collaborate on a 50-50 basis to get their songs completed. This means that they split equally on any royalties their cowritten songs earn. They also share on the expenses of each song's promotion.

Here are some proven ways you can find a collaborator:

1. Attend music conventions. The Country Music Festival, for example, is an ideal place to meet a flock of composers and lyric writers. You can surely find one or more collaborators to work with on new songs at this convention. It's much easier to attend the Country Music Festival (held each October in Nashville) if you have at least one song credit (one published, recorded song) to your name; if you're already working in radio or for a music publication; or if you're connected in some other way with the music business. However, if you know any disc jockeys, they might be able to get you in at the convention. Visitors to the convention pay a set fee, which is subject to change from year to year, to watch some of the program activities held at the downtown auditorium in Nashville.

Even if you cannot get into the convention, it's worth being in Nashville during that week. The town is filled with songwriters (both lyricists and composers), and many of them can be seen strolling around the auditorium area. It's certainly possible to meet some of these music people. It's been done many times before.

2. Another possibility is to visit the offices of music publishers, recording companies, and/or music publications. You can't count on it, but they might be able to suggest someone you can contact about possible collaboration on new songs. To save yourself a trip, write them first.

3. Read the major music publications, like *Billboard,* and watch for ads by other songwriters looking for cowriters. You can then answer the ads that interest you. You should read the major music publications anyway, whether you're looking for a collaborator or not.

4. Another proven way to get a cowriter for your songs is to run an advertisement yourself in one of the key music publications. (*Billboard* and *Cash Box* are two of the best.) Your ad may read: "Wanted: A composer (lyricist) to write the music (lyrics) for writer's new lyric (music)." Be sure to include your name and address. You should receive a number of replies and then can choose which composer you want to try. This method usually works, no matter what type of song you have: rock, pop, country, rhythm and blues, folk songs, novelty, gospel, or show tunes.

5. Write to ASCAP (American Society of Composers, Authors, and Publishers) or BMI (Broadcast Music Incorporated) in New York City for lists of their members who are interested in cowriting on new songs. Bear in mind that they may send these lists to members only. But it's worth a try. After you get one song credit to your name, you're eligible to join either ASCAP or BMI. You could then obtain a list of other writer-members interested in collaborating.

6. Run a classified ad in your hometown newspaper stating that you seek a cowriter. There may be some writing talent closer than you think.

7. Run a classified ad in the Nashville, Tennessee, newspapers stating that you seek a composer or lyricist interested in cowriting on new songs. This way, even if you live far away from Nashville, you might interest a Nashville-based writer in working with you on one of your songs. Once the two of you have a complete song you feel has a good chance, your cowriter is right there on the Nashville scene to promote the song and take it around to publishing-recording offices.

Advantages of Collaboration

Some of the advantages of collaborating with another writer-composer on new songs include the following:

1. It gives you a chance to specialize on either lyrics or music.

2. Your work on the song is over when you finish the lyrics or music. This gives you more time to start on other songs. And you will probably find that you will complete a greater number of songs more quickly than if you were writing both music and lyrics yourself.

3. You have someone to share the expenses of taping, marketing, and promoting your songs.

4. Both you and your cowriter double the promotion on your songs.

5. You may well have twice as many music business contacts. This advantage alone could mean a much better chance of placing your songs for recording.

6. If you and your cowriter live in the same city or area, you can work together on new songs on a regular basis. This is a real plus, because you can kick new ideas around and get each other's reaction at once.

7. The person you cowrite with might be a musician, singer, arranger, or all three. This would make it easier to

produce fairly good demo tapes (demonstrations) of your songs.

Disadvantages of Collaboration

Along with the advantages of working with a cowriter, there are also disadvantages:

1. In cowriting with another, you often have to work by mail. This means extra time is needed to hear from your partner. You also run the risk of losing material and tapes in the mail. When two writers live in two different cities, decision making and communication in general can often be a problem. The most successful writing teams have been those who live in the same city and are able to work together regularly.

2. When you collaborate, you sometimes might have to accept music or lyrics you don't really feel is strong enough.

3. Disagreements can take place over many areas of songwriting: writing itself; getting demo tapes of songs; expenses of promotion; or which companies a song is right for. If there is a disagreement of any kind, it's possible that your cowriter may stop working with you at any time.

4. The royalties on all cowritten songs must be split two ways or more, depending on how many writers are involved.

5. Your cowriter may not agree to the basic contract offered on one or more songs. In other words, you cannot make some decisions without the approval of your cowriter.

6. Cowriting brings up the question of whether you should have a written agreement signed by both you and your collaborator.

Agreements Between Cowriters

Some writers like to have some form of written agreement on file, so that if any disputes should arise between their cowriters and themselves, the agreement protects both parties. There are two approaches regarding agreements between collaborators.

You can both sign a written agreement to share equally in all profits of the songs you create. This agreement could be a formal one drawn up by a lawyer or simply a statement written by you or your cowriter. Some agreements make provision for a time period or a trial period for the collaboration. Who knows? You may find someone else five or ten years (or even six months) from now whom you'd rather work with on new songs. You might also evolve into writing complete songs on your own. So in either case, you would want to be free from any collaboration obligation.

It was said that George M. Cohan, an all-time great songwriter who did both lyrics and music, never signed a contract with his producing-management partner Sam Harris. The two once admitted that the only agreement between them was a handshake. In today's world, it's probably wiser in the long run to have a signed agreement in your files whether or not your cowriter is a very close friend. Even good friends can sometimes come to a parting of the ways, as the song says.

The Right Cowriter Makes All the Difference

With the right cowriter, collaboration on new songs can be a rewarding experience for a songwriter.

When you and your cowriter lock yourselves up for several hours with a piano, guitar, paper, and pens and then emerge with a complete new song (or often only part of a song) it's an enriching experience. It develops your creative powers even more. Any songwriter can of course work alone. Many prefer to write all of their songs by themselves. But working with a cowriter you respect with both of you in complete control of the creative process of each song is something that stays with you. It certainly makes you a more effective songwriter as well as a more sensitive one.

A cowriter who lives in the same area you do and with whom you can work well on new material can accomplish far more. Remember. The cowriter you choose to collaborate with can make a difference in how far you might go in songwriting. You might say that the shortest distance between you and a hit song could be the right collaborator. Choose wisely.

7

How to Protect Your Song

Many songwriters wonder if music publishers, record labels, musicians, and others in the business will try to steal their songs or song ideas. While most companies will treat you fairly and never think of stealing your songs, it still makes sense to protect your material. After all, your songs represent a lot of time and effort on your part as well as money spent on tapes and promotion.

The best form of legal protection for your new songs is a Library of Congress copyright. By completing application form E and sending it with the stated registration fee (plus a copy of your song), you will receive within a few weeks your copy of the certificate of copyright registration. To get a supply of these forms, simply write and request them from the Register of Copyrights, Library of Congress, Washington, D.C., 20540. Form E is required for unpublished and published musical compositions written by citizens.

Song lyrics alone, without music, cannot be copyrighted in *unpublished* form. The copyright law considers and classes lyrics without music as a "book." So a series or collection of lyrics could be published as a book. Once this is done, and the copyright notice appears in the "book" of lyrics, copyright may be obtained. In this way, then, a writer can secure copyright protection for his or her lyrics.

Your copy of the certificate of copyright (on complete songs) will bear the date on which your song was registered with the Library of Congress. This copyright will stand up in any court of law as reliable and acceptable proof that you are the creator of that particular song and that the song was indeed registered at the copyright office on the indicated date.

Extra Protection for Your Songs

Along with a Library of Congress copyright, many song-writers also keep a written record (in a notebook or file) of the dates they first started work on their songs and when the songs were completed. These dates serve as extra protection for you, because they are further evidence that you are the writer-composer of the material.

Another cheaper way to protect the songs you write is simply to mail a copy of your song to yourself by registered mail. When it arrives in the mail, do not open it. Keep it in a safe place and sealed. On the back of the envelope, write the title of the song you have protected in this way for future reference. The idea behind this method is that if you ever need to prove the song is yours, your sealed and registered letter (with your song inside) is good evidence that you're indeed the creator of the song.

If you wish to have still more protection for your songs, you can keep notes and·work-sheets revealing the actual work you did on various songs. All of this material could be kept in file folders with the titles of the particular songs written clearly on them. I use this system myself and have found that it works well. On the copies of songs (the lead sheets) they send to themselves by registered mail, some songwriters write or type their names and addresses on the back. Below their names, they include the date the song was finished and then have two or three witnesses sign their names. Friends, neighbors, or family members can sign as witnesses. These signatures of witnesses will serve as still further evidence that you are the creator of the songs.

In most cases, a Library of Congress copyright will be ample protection for your songs. However, if you want more (and many writers do), by all means take some of these extra protection steps. The more sources of evidence you can produce in court that you are the creator of a song, the more likely it will be proved in your favor. You may never have to appear in court regarding your songs, but if you do, you'll be well prepared.

Remember. A song copyright is simply a dated registration of your song with the Library of Congress in Washington, D.C. You state on the form you send to Washington that you wrote the song. Give your cowriter's name and address, if the song was cowritten. Be sure to include the title and your address in the indicated places on the copyright application form. Send the completed form with a neat copy of your song (a professional looking lead sheet is fine), and you'll soon receive your copyright certificate. Don't forget to send the proper fee for *each* song copyright.

How Many Songs Should You Copyright?

Whatever your total number of new songs turns out to be for any year, you'll have to decide how many to copyright. A good rule I follow, myself, is to carefully choose the songs I feel have the best commercial chances to be recorded and make money, even if it amounts to only two or three songs. I copyright only these songs.

The odds are that you'll have to write a lot of songs for every real gem you produce. You can take the other steps already mentioned for protection on your other songs.

Common Law Protection

Even before your songs are accepted by a publisher or recording company, they are fully protected as unpublished works under the common law. This law prohibits the use of your unpublished songs (or other works) without your permission. If your songs are copied, published, or used without your knowledge and consent, you're entitled to damages.

The Copyright Notice

If your songs are copyrighted, there are three elements that are required to appear on the lead sheets or copies, These are:

1. The word "Copyright" or the copyright symbol: ©
2. The name of the copyright owner.
3. The year of publication.

For example:

© John Smith—1977
Copyright 1977—by John Smith

Songwriters who are U. S. citizens may secure automatic protection in many other countries overseas by using the following type of copyright notice:

© John Smith—1977
All Rights Reserved

What Cannot Be Copyrighted?

1. Song titles cannot be copyrighted.

2. Sound recordings, including records and tape recordings. They're not considered to be "copies."

3. Mottos.

4. Toys and games (they're protected by patents).

5. Publications of the U.S. Government.

More Money and Protection for Songwriters

By the time you read these words in print, a new copyright law should have been passed by Congress and in effect. It is long overdue. The new law will extend the copyright period of protection to the life of an author plus 50 years. This new law will also require, for the first time, that jukeboxes, cable television, and public broadcasting pay royalties on the songs and music used.

8

Good Demos Are a Must

One of the best investments for your songwriting career is a good demo of your song. Demos are discs, reel-to-reel tape recordings, or tape cassettes that demonstrate what your song sounds like. Good demos are a must in today's music business, if your songs are going to have their best chance to compete with all the others.

When earlier songwriters like George M. Cohan, George Gershwin, Gus Kahn, and many others were building their careers, it was customary to play and sing a song "live" in a publisher's office. That was the day when sheet music was king of the music industry. Publishing firms made most of their money from sheet music sales at that time.

The accent today is on records. A song has little chance of going very far in today's music scene until it's commercially recorded and released. What does this mean to you as a songwriter? It means that you have to get record releases of your song, and the more the better. Your songs must be recorded and get radio spins before they can start making money for you.

It's usually wiser to use reel-to-reel tapes for your song demos. While an increasing number of music publishers can listen to your new songs either on discs or tape cassettes, the majority of them prefer reel-to-reel tape demos. You can of course use all three if you wish. It's a frustrating experience to arrive at a publisher's office with a song you want them to hear only to find out that they have no way to play a cassette or disc.

The Quality of Your Demos

Unless you've had some experience in making demos, be cautious about which demo company handles your material. There are plenty of demo firms in the country. Most of them are located in the three major recording centers: Nashville, New York, and Hollywood. It's a good idea to request a sample of a company's demo quality before ordering any demos. Also, be sure that you understand how many musical instruments a firm's demo price actually covers.

Some demo outfits have angered professional songwriters either by failing to do songs in the style asked for or by just doing poor quality demos in general. If at all possible, check out a demo company in person—and be there in person when your song demos are cut.

High quality demos can run hundreds of dollars and up depending on who does them, how many instruments you want, special effects desired, and other factors. Remember, a poor demo can ruin a basically good song, while a fine demo sometimes can help a mediocre song's chances to be accepted. Most publishers make their decisions completely on what they hear when they listen to your song demo.

How Many Songs Should You Demo?

How many of your songs deserve effective demos? You'll have to answer this question sooner or later. Most songwriters cannot afford to get expensive demos on many of their songs. Get demos only on the very best songs you write. You could get lower-priced demos on your other songs or even do home-produced tapes on them yourself.

If you average about fifty new songs a year, for example, you're obviously going to have to decide which songs you think have the strongest chance for success. Songwriters are often poor judges of their own work. Many writers have had high-priced demos cut on the wrong songs, leaving some of your best numbers without any demos at all. The songs you like yourself may not be the ones that the publishers will like.

So try to be objective and select songs to demo that you feel have the very best commercial chances. A lot of writers choose what they feel are their four or five best songs written during any given year. They get good demos on these carefully selected songs. You may eventually write five, fifty, or 300 songs a year. But the odds are very much against more than several of them becoming money-making songs. Even long established name writers have admitted that it usually takes about fifty or so songs to get one real hit. With lots of experience, some successful writers have reduced the odds to about one in twenty, while others have written hundreds and hundreds of songs before they got their first hit.

A Word About Masters

A master is usually thought of as an actual recording session on your song—the full treatment with top musicians, a good arrangement, artist, and any desired background singers or effects. Prices for a master begin at a few thousand dollars and up. However, once you have a master of your song in hand, you might be able to sell it to a record company. The beauty of a master is that records can be pressed from it.

It happens occasionally in the business that some high-priced demos on songs turn out so well that they may be called master demos. The demo isn't really a master in the full meaning of the term, but the quality achieved may be very close to a master. Unless you have the money to finance masters of your songs, focus your attention on getting the best demos you can for the most reasonable prices. As you become more experienced you may want to have masters produced on your very best songs.

Do-It-Yourself Demos

A great many writers do their own song demos at home, using a tape recorder and a guitar or piano. The idea is that some type of demo is better than no demo at all. Some writers like to hear the way their new songs sound on tape and then experiment with them. If you can't sing or play well enough to get a basic demo of your song, you should have little trouble finding someone to play and/or sing your song on tape for a small fee.

The cheaper type of song demo is a business in itself. There are many lower-priced demo companies around. They are often just individuals offering simple voice and guitar-piano demos. The prices charged are often as low as $15 and up.

With a basic demo of your song, even a fairly crude one, you can decide later to get a better demo produced. Meanwhile, you have your song on tape to listen to, re-do, and develop if you wish.

A number of publishers have told writers personally that their main interest is how the music and lyrics come together and that "a fancy demo is not necessary." Many publishers don't really care if a demo is just a simple voice and guitar-piano rendition of the song. If the song is there, some of them evidently believe it will come across. And of course publishers may produce a new demo on their own.

But why push your luck in a highly competitive song business? Get the best demos you possibly can on your songs. The music business is much more than just writing new songs; it's also selling, marketing, advertising, and exploiting those songs. A good quality demo can only help your song, so make up your mind now to give your songs the best demo presentation you can manage. It will pay off for you in the long run with more song placements.

9

Three Major Markets for Your Songs

The big day has arrived. You've written what you feel are one or more hit songs and you have strong demos on them. What do you do next? The world will never hear your new songs unless you get them to the right markets.

The three key markets for your material are music publishers, record companies, and recording artists.

Music Publishers Can Get Records on Your Songs

One of the best markets for your songs is a reliable music publisher. Placing your material with the right publisher can quickly open songwriting doors for you. In a real sense, a music publisher acts as an agent for you. A publisher's goal is the same as yours—one or more commercial record releases of your songs. Successful music publishers go after as many records as they can get for the songs on their roster.

Publishers can usually do better than a songwriter in

seeking records on songs because they have valuable contacts with recording company executives developed over the years. Many songwriters are unable to see the man who makes the decisions at an important record label. Of course, after a writer gets some hits, it becomes increasingly easier to see executives and A & R (Artists and Repertoire) directors with the power to record your songs.

Paul Williams, a very talented and successful writer, says that finding a publisher for your song is most important. "It's the first and basic step. Where a song goes after it's published depends on record company executives."

Paul also advises writers to be prepared before seeing a publisher by having a lead sheet and typed copy of the lyrics. "If you can, have a demo tape and keep it simple. A song can be orchestrated and arranged after it's published."

Sources of Reputable Music Publishers

A good way to get a list of reputable music publishers is to write ASCAP and BMI in New York City. Both organizations maintain lists of their publisher affiliates.

A faster way to get lists of music publishers is to write them down yourself from current Nashville, New York, and Hollywood telephone Yellow Page directories. If you use an old phone directory for such a list, the addresses of some publishers may not be up-to-date. Accurate publisher lists are also frequently offered for sale by various companies that advertise in song lyric magazines and other music trade publications. These lists you pay for will also usually include record label addresses. Lists of recording artist addresses are also sometimes offered by mail.

The Right Way to Contact Music Publishers

It's far better, if at all possible, to see a music publisher in person about your song . . . rather than to send it by mail.

Here are four basic steps that have helped many writers place their songs. Use them as a guide in contacting publishers.

1. Try to keep up with what songs are being handled successfully by what publishers. Watching the song popularity charts will tell you which publishers seem to be getting the most and the most important record releases.

2. Do your best to match your song with the publisher it seems to fit the most. The winning combination is the right song for the right publisher at the right time.

3. Write the publisher you've chosen and request an appointment with the firm's professional manager. If you can find out the manager's name before writing, so much the better. Many writers address their letters to the president of a company. A specific name on your envelope is always better. You can of course phone for an appointment, but a letter usually works better.

4. Be at the company's office at least five minutes before your appointment. Come prepared with a neat lead sheet, typed lyric copy, and a demo tape of your song. Never try to interest a publisher in more than two or three songs at one time. If you show you're professional in this manner and that you value the publisher's time, the door of that company will be open to you for future attempts to place songs.

Never be discouraged by a music publisher's rejection. If you're a real songwriter—or intend to be—make up your mind now to never let a music publisher's rejection of your song or songs get you down. And never take one publisher's reaction or opinion as final. The next one who hears your song may like it.

Keep in mind that music publishers are human too. While their decisions are right most of the time, they do make mistakes. Some of them have made some whoppers over the years. Some of the biggest publishers in the business turned down "Heartbreak Hotel," the huge Elvis Presley hit. They didn't think the song was hit material.

Still other key publishers turned thumbs down on one of the top song hits of this century, "I Left My Heart in San Francisco." The story goes that the writers of this song tried for eight years to place it. Music publishers turned them down time after time. But they refused to give up on the song. It was eventually accepted and later recorded by Tony Bennett. The rest is song history.

Cole Porter, the brilliant Broadway writer-composer, was told in the early days of his career by music publishers that his songs were "too good . . . not commercial . . . too sophisticated."

In fairness to music publishers, it should be pointed out that a number of them have gone out of their way to help writers. They are businessmen with excellent knowledge and experience in the industry. In most cases, their judgement and final decisions are sound. The better publishers have almost daily contact with major recording companies. They can be of enormous help to you in getting your songs launched and recorded.

In dealing with publishers be courteous and businesslike; be professional in all your contacts with them, and value their time. Don't let a publisher discourage you. If one breaks or doesn't keep an appointment or if he fails to answer your letters requesting an appointment, try another publisher. There are bound to be some right publishers for your songs. Finding them is the challenge and this can be done by keeping up with what's happening in the industry. In time, you should begin to get a feel as to which publishers might be the right ones for you.

The major publishers have staff writers under contract turning out new songs for them on a regular basis. This means that you've got to hit publishers with material that is fresh, different, and stronger than what their exclusive writers may be supplying and bringing to them.

Recording Companies as a Market

Some songwriters bypass the music publisher and take their songs to a recording company. There are reasons for trying it this way. A number of writers have formed their own publishing companies and naturally seek records on their songs. A writer may have some good contacts with one or more labels. Or a writer may simply prefer to deal directly with a recording company. The major record labels usually have their own publishing company wings, so there's no problem if a label likes your material.

Unless you have an inside contact or already have a proven track record of recorded song credits, you may find that the major labels will refer you back to music publishers. Some top recording executives even reply by form letter to songwriters who have written the labels about their songs. This form letter urges a songwriter to first interest a publisher in his or her material.

But record companies can be a market for your songs, provided you can sell them on using your material. If you manage to obtain a well-produced master for one of your songs, you should have little trouble getting at least a fair listen at the major labels. Record companies are looking for hits and they frankly don't care where they come from or who wrote them.

What A & R Directors Seek

The A & R Directors at various recording labels have well-defined objectives. They know what they want. Those especially interested in reaching the mass market with their firm's records seek new (and even strange) sounds. Such sounds may be far from what you're accustomed to thinking of as musical. Young people today still buy most of the pop records. Melody or tone quality may mean something quite different to them from what they mean to you.

The questions an A & R director asks are whether a given song will sell a lot of records. Will the song hit the mass market where they live? Is the sound different and appealing? To interest an A & R director in your songs, your material has got to be different, hard-hitting, and possibly even primitive (for the pop market). By knowing what kind of market an A & R executive is trying to reach (and with what artists), you'll have a much better idea of what songs to audition for him. The rock hit, "Goin' Out of My Head," must have made any record label that first heard the song sit up and listen hard.

Don't Forget Recording Artists
If a record label and publisher turn your song down, you don't have to throw up your hands and quit. Do what you can to interest any and all recording artists who you think are right for the song in your material.

Some disagree that recording artists should be thought of as a market for songs. They say that most record label artists have little or no control over the songs they record and perform. This may be true in the case of many singers, but an artist can certainly put in a plug for a song he or she likes and can express interest in recording it. Because of this influence and the contacts an artist has, he or she shouldn't be ruled out as a market for your songs.

Even if a recording artist has no choice on the songs to be used, that same artist might be able to pass the song along to another singer-performer who can use it. Singers switch record labels from time to time, tour the country and the world, and have friends in the major entertainment centers. They get to know a variety of people in the music business. If they like a song and decide to go to bat for it, they could certainly be of help in getting your song to the right people.

In one of her concert appearances in Memphis, country singer Lynn Anderson told the audience that a Memphis songwriter had sent her a new song she liked. With a cue to her musicians, she then sang the song. It was warmly received. An introduction like this by a name artist can help launch a writer's song and his career. But it would never have happened if the song hadn't been sent to Lynn Anderson in the first place. There's no assurance an artist will like or do anything with your song. But there's always the chance.

Sometimes the manager of an artist will urge that singer to use a certain song. He may also suggest who you might try with it. You can personally contact artists at the night clubs, hotels, and theaters where they appear. Las Vegas is a good place to try to contact them because there are usually so many artists in town at the same time. Other writers are doing just that. You may not get near enough to speak to them, but you can try.

Some additional—though less important—markets for your songs are included in Chapter 12. You should be aware of these other chances to place your songs. A number of them can be very helpful in getting your songs launched.

10

Making the Rounds Yourself Versus Mailing Your Songs

The songwriter who lives in or near one of the major recording centers has a distinct advantage over those who must send their song material by mail. Writers who are able to get to Nashville, Hollywood, Memphis, or New York a few times a year are also better off than those who must rely totally on the mail.

Disadvantages of Mailing Songs to Markets

It's true that a number of songwriters have placed some of their songs by mail. But for the most part, using the mail to try to place your songs is a gamble at best. Here are some of the major disadvantages:

1. The U. S. Postal Service has increasingly been called unreliable. Your songs may be lost and never arrive at a publishing or recording company office.

2. Your demo tapes and lead sheets (plus typed lyrics)

may be damaged and torn going through the mail. Any writer who has used the mail often can attest to this. If your songs get where they are going and/or back to you, your material may arrive looking like it was left overnight on a freeway.

3. Your material may not be returned. A writer is supposed to enclose a self-addressed stamped folder for the return of rejected songs. But some music firms are downright careless about sending material back even when the writer has paid for it. Reliable companies do try to return all material, but mistakes can and do happen. Companies are often swamped with songs sent in, and sometimes a writer loses his material or gets somebody else's song back.

4. It is difficult to make good contacts in the business by mail. There's no personal connection with a name.

5. The larger and more important the company is, the greater the chance your song demo may wind up in a huge stack with hundreds of others.

6. The songs you send may arrive at the worst possible time. The person who makes the decisions may be out of town, ill, or too busy to hear your material.

7. You can't be sure who will be the one to listen to your songs. Some companies have been known to let their janitors listen to tapes that arrive by mail.

8. You're not there on the scene to get immediate reaction to your songs. This is a big disadvantage. Reasons your material is rejected are usually not given by mail. You may only receive a form rejection slip. You have very little chance to find out . . . by mail . . . if your song or songs even came close. It's certainly helpful to know where your material missed the mark, so you can do better next time.

9. Some top-rated writers and composers have advised against sending songs in by mail. This alone is a strong reason for not using the mail.

It's possible of course that your songs sent in by mail may eventually be either accepted or returned to you. But the disadvantages are strong reasons not to send in the songs you've spent time, effort, and probably money on as well.

If you become a fairly active writer and eventually have a number of well-produced demo tapes or masters available for placement, you run the risk of losing half or all of your expensive demos by sending them through the mail. This has happened to many writers and it can be a serious loss.

The Case for Making the Rounds in Person

Some people in the music game feel strongly that a songwriter isn't really a songwriter until he or she has made the rounds of publishing offices in New York, Los Angeles, Nashville, or Memphis.

There's no doubt about it. The ideal way to try to place your songs is to take them with you in person to the offices of recording companies and publishers. Here are four steps to follow:

1. Make appointments with publishers and record companies that you believe are reliable.

2. Take your material—demo tapes, lead sheets, and lyrics—with you to their offices.

3. Request that your songs be played-auditioned in your presence. If they won't listen to them while you are there, you certainly don't have to leave them. Try another company.

4. If rejected, try to find out where your songs missed the mark. If you respect the company and feel you were treated fairly, keep the door open to try again later.

Writer and recording artist Linda Hargrove first tries to interest an artist in her songs. "I think the more successful writers take their songs around." There are many other writers in the country field who agree with her.

Here are some direct advantages of making the rounds yourself with your songs:

1. You have a better chance to sell your song in person. Salesmanship has helped place a lot of songs.

2. Going in person is faster and far more professional.

3. The music companies, labels, producers, and, possibly, artists will get to know you and be able to connect your face with your name.

4. You may meet other writers and recording artists while waiting for your appointment.

5. You learn the song business better and faster by making the rounds in person.

6. You will get the reaction to your songs at once. There's no long delay or wondering when you'll hear something by mail.

7. Sometimes a publisher will offer specific suggestions to re-do a song. A writer who is not there in person would miss this chance.

8. You get current, up-to-date knowledge of the type of material different companies want.

9. You have a 100 percent better chance to be in the right place, at the right time, and maybe with the right song.

10. You learn the importance of contacts in building your career as a songwriter.

11. You'll worry less about your material because you're there in person while it's being auditioned.

When you go in person with your songs, you usually get faster attention. There's always the chance a publishing or recording executive will take a liking to you and try to help you by offering advice or suggestions about your songs.

Once you make contact with a few good publishers or

labels, get to know their song needs, and obtain their okay (their personal okay) to submit future songs. You may then send in new material regularly by mail. This is the way some individual writers and teams of writers work.

Jerry Foster and Bill Rice, one of the most successful cowriting teams of today, got started this same way. The two met at a Missouri radio station back in 1959 and began writing songs in 1961. They found a reliable publisher in Nashville to send material to regularly. According to Foster, "We sent him an awful lot of songs, but only a few of them were worth anything." That changed, however, with time. Their publisher began to get more and more of their songs recorded. Both writers are reported to be millionaires today with over 1,000 songs to their credit. The walls of their Nashville office are covered with awards and plaques for their songs.

It may take awhile to establish a reliable outlet for your songs, so, until you do, make the rounds in person.

Trying by Mail Is Better Than Nothing

For many writers who are unable to go in person to the recording centers, trying by mail is better than no efforts at all. Songs are accepted by mail; but realize what you're up against and try to deal only with highly professional companies.

If at all possible, at least strive to make a few rounds in person to set up a dependable outlet for your songs. Then you can send your songs by mail continually with the assurance that they'll receive proper attention (as Foster and Rice did in the early stages of their writing).

There are many professional writers who combine methods to place their songs, that is, they mail their songs as well as make the rounds. Some also hire agents to sell their songs. If one method works well, try adding other methods to increase your chances of placing songs.

A writer once mailed the late Johnny Mercer the first

several lines of a lyric idea. Johnny liked the idea, and the result was a hit song called "I Wanna Be Around." That writer receives to this day about $3,000 a year in royalties. So selling songs through the mail can work. This kind of break doesn't happen often, however.

11

Your First Song Contract

It's a happy day when you're offered a contract on one of your songs. Many of today's established writers still remember the day they signed their first contract. With your signature on that first contract, you feel like you're on your way. And you may be, especially if it's a standard contract with one of the better companies.

After your feet have touched down again on Mother Earth, there are things to consider about song contracts in general. Most writers are so happy and pleased to get their first contract that they're just about certain to sign it and hope for the best. This is understandable. But from then on, you would be wise to keep some basic truths about song contracts in mind.

Make no mistake about it. Contracts in themselves mean little to you, as a songwriter, unless and until they result in a commercial record release. There are fine writers around the country with stacks of contracts in their files.

These contracts did not result in the songs actually being recorded and released. You cannot make money from your songs until they are recorded, released, and doing well in the stores and on radio.

Why does this happen? Why do contracts sometimes turn out to be useless? Well, the publisher who took your song may be a small company or a new company that may go out of business. Perhaps your publisher was unable to get a record company to record your song. Publishers and record labels also change their minds about using some songs. If the song needed to be released within a certain period of time to ride the crest of a news item—an election, the public interest, a fad—events could quickly date a song.

The Importance of a Time Clause

When you're offered a contract, one of the first things to check is whether it has a time clause. Some contracts include them. Others don't. A time clause is just that: a clause in a song contract stating that if your publisher doesn't get a record of your song within a certain period of time (six months, one year, or longer), the song reverts back to you, the writer.

You'd be surprised how many trusting songwriters have signed contracts without any time clause in them. It's like handing your song over to a company for an indefinite period of time. Some companies take a long time to take any action on songs, or never act at all. Unless you plan to be here during the next century, resolve now to always request the insertion of a time clause in any song contract you sign. It's more professional and also makes good sense.

If a publisher really wants your song, he shouldn't object to your request for a one-year time clause. Try to get a six-months time limit if you can. If not, you can settle for one year. If a company hasn't gotten a recording on your song after a year, it may be a wise move to offer your song to another market. Maybe your publisher isn't trying very hard for a recording. Many songwriters with good contacts and some credits to their names sometimes are able to get their new material recorded in two or three days. However, most writers will have to be more patient.

Unfortunately, there are some companies that take songs from writers, issue contracts, and then let the songs sit on a shelf in their office. Either they are too busy getting records on the songs of their own staff writers or they lose interest in the material. They may also be unable to get a firm recording commitment but don't wish to return the song rights to the writer. You can't afford to tie up some of your best songs for years. There are too many other markets out there that might be able to record your material within weeks or a few months. By developing good contacts, talking to other writers, and studying the music trade publications, you should be able to tell what companies are actually getting record releases on new songs.

Don't Sign Song Contracts Too Quickly

Unless you know for a fact that the company you're dealing with is reputable (through previous experience, inside information, or the contacts you have), take some time to study over any contracts that you're offered. Many writers have a lawyer look over their contracts.

I was so eager to sign my first song contract years ago (with a small and relatively unknown company) that I lost out on a direct offer from another publisher to have my song recorded on a major label (Atlantic Records). If the publishing rights hadn't been tied up, my very first contracted song could have landed on a major label. I learned from this experience that a writer must be careful with whom he deals and what kind of contract he signs. There are different types of contracts in the business, and some are better and fairer than others.

The Meaning of a Contract

A song contract is basically just a written agreement stating that a writer assigns a certain song to a publisher for a period of time. Cash advances used to be common in the business many years ago. There are few, if any, advances offered today. Only top writers may occasionally receive an advance.

Royalty provisions are included in contracts, in the event the material is commercially recorded and marketed. Some of these stated amounts to be paid include royalties for piano copies and orchestrations (U.S. and foreign), song lyric folio use of the song, sheet music, 50 percent of the proceeds received on the mechanical rights of the song (records, television, films), and other stipulated royalties. Contracts vary, of course, in the amount of the royalty payments for songs.

One very important royalty provision in a contract is that of performance rights. If a song clicks, it may be recorded many times by different labels and artists. It may also receive a lot of performances on radio (record spins) and television. These public performances for profit can all add up to a lot of money over a period of years. Try to hold out for 50 percent of the performance rights split.

An Organization That Protects Writers

If you find contracts confusing you might wish to join the American Guild of Authors and Composers. This New York organization, formerly called the Songwriters' Protective Association, is dedicated to better protection for writers regarding the contracts they sign. The organization helps writers get fairer contracts, countersigns them after approval, and requires a time clause (or release) and the return of a song if a publisher cannot obtain a recording on it within a set period of time.

There's no need to consider joining AGAC, however, until you're placing many songs and find yourself knee-deep in contracts. You could contact them at that time for full information on their services to writers.

Never Pay to Have Your Songs Published

Honest and professional music publishers do not charge a writer for publishing his or her songs. There are unethical companies on the fringe of the business that charge writers for various so-called song services, music for lyrics, $300 and up for "test recording sessions," and other gimmicks designed to fleece songwriters. Beware of these sharks. It's often difficult to bring legal action against them, because of their crafty legal interpretations. They prey on the inexperienced, unknown writer. They may rave over your song to get you enthused about dealing with them. Check a publisher out first with the Better Business Bureau, and never pay to be published.

There are many honest companies that offer legitimate services for the songwriter: demos, lead sheets, tape duplication service, lists of artists, record labels, publishers, and other items that can help writers. All these services are those for which you should expect to pay.

Mrs. Evelyn Graves, of the Memphis Songwriters Association, advises writers never to pay a publisher. "If a publisher believes in a song, he pays the songwriter. If a publisher asks you for money, chances are you are being cheated." Various recording executives, lawyers, and songwriters in the major music centers back up her advice.

No ethical publisher advertises for lyrics or music for songs, so be especially wary of ads in certain magazines soliciting lyrics for musical setting.

Don't let the song sharks of the music industry get their

teeth into you. We would hate to lose you as a songwriter. After all, you may have the next hit.

12

Ways to Promote Your Songs

Many of today's successful writers wear numerous hats. The industry today is more oriented to the total entertainer, talented individuals or musical groups who can write, perform, and produce new material.

Paul Anka is a good example of today's era of the artist-performer-writer-musician. He's a fantastic songwriter, excellent musician, and proven singer-performer. But even Paul Anka was an unknown at one time. He wasn't content to stay in his native Canada and send his songs to New York. He hit the big town himself while still in his teens and sold his first hit, "Diana," in person. The song sold over eight million copies. He's gone a long way since the day he first sang "Diana" for a recording executive. "A lot of times now it's just a matter of sitting down with the people who run the industry, the people who are the pockets of power, and deciding what you can offer for what price," he says.

Your Songs Deserve Promotion

There are few writers who are artist-performer-writer-musician. But for most songwriters, there may be at least a few other areas of the business they could learn more about and thus add to their total understanding of the business.

Even songwriters who are able to work at their writing only part-time can do more to help their songs along. They can promote their material before and after it's recorded and released. Some publishers may not be as aware of the value of promotion as others. So any promotion you do on your own could be of real help to your songs.

A lot of writers say they prefer to concentrate on writing songs and to leave the marketing and promotion matters up to their publisher or record label. These writers, however, are established and are able to spend most of their working days on their writing.

A new songwriter should get out and promote his new releases. The publishers and labels are unlikely to object to extra promotion. Even good songs need all the promotion they can get, to have the best possible chance to compete.

The decision to promote on your own, or not to promote, may well depend on who has your songs and how actively they seem to be working on them.

If your songs are accepted, recorded, and eventually released, they certainly deserve to be promoted. You may not have the money, solid music contacts, and promotion knowledge of a major company, but there are positive things you can do on your own to call attention to your songs and give them a better chance to reach the public and do well.

Learn More About Song Promotion

The art of song or record promotion is an important phase of the music business. And you can certainly learn more about it over a period of time. Len Levy, a 25-year veteran of the music business, believes that "record companies should offer training programs in various areas of the business." Promotion would certainly be one of those areas.

P. T. Barnum, the showman and brilliant promoter of the last century, left a guide for success that is valuable to songwriters. One of his rules is "to be systematic—to have a time and place for everything." A proven system of better organization is to list each night the things, in order of their importance, you must do the next day to keep your songwriting career advancing and moving toward the success you want.

"Advertise your business" is also a must, said Barnum. You can advertise your new record releases and also promote them in a number of ways. If Barnum believed strongly in advertising in the 1870s, you can see how important it is today.

A final pointer is worth noting from Barnum's guide: "Whatever you do, do with all your might." In other words, call on all your powers to reach your goal in songwriting. Be determined. There's great power in a determined person.

How to Promote Your Songs and Records

Here are some specific steps you can take to promote your songs before and after they are recorded:

1. Personally contact local singers and musical groups in your city or home town area. Many of them are trying to build their own careers in music and may be glad to use some of your songs. (This is often an excellent way to get free demos of your songs.)

2. Contact the producers of off-Broadway shows and nightclub entertainment. They may be able to use one of your songs.

3. Contact the following groups who produce amateur theatrical entertainment. There's always a chance they can use one or more of your songs:

    a. Schools and colleges.

    b. Civic clubs—Rotary, Lions, Kiwanis, Chamber of Commerce.

    c. Fraternities and sororities.

    d. Church groups.

4. Talk to festival groups, historical societies, and others planning commemorative plays and pageants. They may be glad to have some original songs.

5. Contact commercial and industrial moviemakers about your song material. Even an entire movie can be created around a song today, as "Ode to Billie Joe" proved.

6. Choral groups, musical instrument societies, and other special groups in your area may be able to use one or more of your songs.

7. Local advertising agencies and business firms that use musical jingles may be a good bet. The jingle field is big business today, and it uses the talents of many who can write motivating lyrics and effective music.

8. Whenever one of your songs is recorded and released, visit radio station DJ's in the surrounding area. Present them with copies of your record and ask for some on-the-air spins. It's important to meet as many key DJ's as possible. Many of them have excellent contacts in the industry and could be of help to you. There are laws against DJ's accepting "payola" today for plugging records over the air. But you can certainly use the principles of good salesmanship to get your records played. And if the DJ's like your records, they may play them often.

9. Ask your friends and relatives to send telegrams to radio stations requesting that your record be played. I once returned to my school music class to promote one of my

recorded songs. My former music teacher introduced me to the class and had me explain how I wrote the song. Later that same afternoon I received a phone call telling me to listen to a key radio statio at a certain time. To my delight my record was played at that time. During the weeks that followed, my record received many additional spins on several stations. The music class had chipped in and sent a telegram requesting to hear my song. Not many DJ's can ignore the request of an entire class of students.

10. Promote your songs through newspapers. Papers use such items, because of the local interest. Getting your name and latest recorded release mentioned can stimulate the sales of your record and help build your songwriting career.

11. If you can afford it you could finance a professional master on the song in a key recording center. Most large and small record labels buy master tapes from individuals or other companies. This can be a faster way to get results with a song.

12. Persuade someone to back you and your songs. If you can succeed in doing this, your future in the music business might well be assured. Alexander Graham Bell persuaded Queen Victoria to install telephones in her palace, and the rest of the world followed her example. Bell's future was made.

13. Start a blitz campaign to contact personally every recording artist-performer who comes to town. Try to make appointments with these singers or their managers to audition your song demos. Keep in mind, however, that some singers have little control over the new songs they record. But they might be able to use your song in their personal appearances.

14. Compile your own special list of recording company executives. Pick A & R directors from only those labels that you feel are the right ones for your kind of songs. If you

cannot get personal appointments with them, send them the best song demos you have by mail. You might suggest a recording artist or two of theirs who would do the song well. If you have any recorded song credits to your name, be sure to let them know it.

15. When you have a record released, let your publisher know that you'll be glad to help to promote it. This prevents your new record release from being lost in the shuffle of hundreds of new ones that arrive every week at radio stations across the country.

16. Arrange to have your friends and relatives asking for your record at record stores and outlets in your area. Record stores hesitate to order copies of new records until they believe the public will buy them. And record distributors are more apt to push a record if they believe it has wide public appeal.

17. Each year your total combined effort—personal contact, efforts by mail, use of agents—should amount to between 100 and 200 song submissions.

18. Rewrite your old songs that almost made it and create a new promotion campaign for each one.

19. When you reach the point that your songs are frequently being recorded and played on the air, you might consider starting your own music publishing company. Once you have some good contacts with artists and producers, you might be able to do well as a publisher-writer combination. After all, if an artist or producer likes your song, why couldn't you be the publisher? It's the song that counts.

The promotion you do for your own songs and records gives you more chances to be in the right place, at the right time, and will teach you more about the fascinating music business while enabling you to make valuable contacts in the industry. In a real sense, you'll be promoting your career as a songwriter and not just songs and records.

13

What It Takes to Write a Hit

People from all walks of life are interested in the art and craft of songwriting. They often ask questions about what it takes to write a hit song. Here are some of the most frequently asked questions:

Q. How much money can a big hit song make today?
A. It varies, of course, but a big hit can rake in from $75,000 to $100,000 and even more for a super hit.

Q. Can a hit song be written anywhere and just about anytime?
A. Well, Paul Anka wrote his super hit "My Way" on a rainy morning in New York. He wrote the song at 3 A.M. in a hotel room.

Q. Are the odds too great against an unknown writer coming up with a hit?
A. New writers come up with hits all the time. Even suc-

cessful writers and established publishers find it difficult to guess what the public will like next. New writers are often able to create something fresh and different. Every famous writer of today was once an unknown.

Q. Should I write alone or collaborate?
A. It depends on you. After you've written for awhile, you will know if you are best at lyrics, music, or both.

Q. What ingredients make a hit song?
A. It's quite a recipe. Simplicity is vital. So is emotional impact and a melody that glides along without sudden jumps. The lyric must be easily sung. The song as a whole should be unforgettable and up-to-date. It should be written with the market of today in mind. It should have a strong title that sticks in the listener's mind. A study of hit songs reveals a basic appeal to universal desires. "The Green Green Grass of Home" is a good example. The theme of the importance of home is universal. More could be said about this recipe. Creating a hit can be an elusive thing. But that's part of the challenge and fascination of songwriting.

Q. What's the best preparation for a young person shooting for a career as a professional songwriter?
A. The president of a large eastern university once said to a group of young people: "Try different jobs in your twenties, for even if you go from one field to another, you'll eventually find yourself." A liberal arts college education is good preparation in the long run. College may hurt the natural ability of some budding songwriters, but it will probably help the majority. Different jobs in your early years will add to your experience, and this can only help. Novelist and short story writer John O'Hara was a ship steward, railroad clerk,

gas meter reader, amusement park guard, evaluating engineer, soda jerk, and press agent during his early years. One of his longer jobs was that of reporter on Pennsylvania and New York newspapers. He later found fulfillment as a very successful novelist.

Q. Can someone who likes and writes poetry also write commercial songs?

A. Rod McKuen has done both with mind-boggling success. He's the composer of 1,500 songs that have sold more than 180 million records ("Love's Been Good to Me," "Rock Gently," "If You Go Away," "Jean"). His poetry books have sold an astounding 16 million books. It's rare, however, to find someone who can do so well at both.

Q. Should a serious songwriter live in one of the major recording centers?

A. If a writer is in songwriting for the long pull, it naturally helps to live in Nashville, New York, Memphis, or Hollywood. The reason it helps is because you're where it's happening. It's far easier to make some solid contacts with publishers, producers, recording companies, and artists if you're in the same area. But if you can write good songs, it really doesn't make any difference where you live. Once you have one or more reliable outlets for your material, you can send your songs in from anywhere. You can always move to a recording center after your career is launched.

Q. Should I try to write a lot of songs or just a few very good ones?

A. Many writers find that they have to produce a lot of songs to get one of quality. Some writers try for at least one song a day four or five days a week. You'll have to experiment to discover your pace of production.

Q. Can a hit song be written quickly?

A. "Give Him Love" was written in less than 30 minutes. It has been said that Roger Miller wrote "Dang Me" in five minutes. "King of the Road" took a good deal more time. With only the title to start with, Sammy Cahn wrote the first several lines of "Three Coins in the Fountain" and his cowriter had a melody 30 minutes later. The song turned out to be one of their most successful and won an Oscar in 1954. It all depends on the writer. Some songwriters turn out top songs in less than an hour. Others may spend weeks or even months working on a song. Some songs seem to write themselves faster than others.

Q. What advice would you give someone who wants a career as a musician?

A. Make music your life. Get as good as you can, and then try to join a musical group. Trumpet man Doc Severinsen got his early experience and informal training with the big bands of Benny Goodman, Tommy Dorsey, and Charlie Barnett. When television came along, Doc joined NBC as a staff musician.

Q. If an idea for a song keeps nagging at a writer, is this a clue that it might be a hit?

A. It might be. Novelist Jacqueline Susann said that "a writer writes because an idea drives you so much that you have to get it on paper." This is sometimes the case for songwriters. On the other hand, a song may need a lot of changes before it has a chance to become a hit.

Q. Should a writer specialize in one basic type of song or write all kinds of material?

A. In order to specialize, most writers have to first try writing different kinds of songs to discover where their strengths lie. The type of songs you prefer to listen to may give you a clue.

Q. What would you say is the single most important thing needed to come up with a hit song?

A. Perseverance. Goethe, the German poet and dramatist, once wrote that "there are but two roads that lead to an important goal and to the doing of great things: strength and perseverance. Strength is the lot of but a few privileged men, but austere perseverance, harsh and continuous, may be employed by the smallest of us and rarely fails of its purpose, for its silent power grows irresistibly greater with time."

Glen Sherley spent more than eleven years in California prisons before being paroled to the custody of country music star Johnny Cash. Sherley got interested in songwriting while in prison and stuck with it. When Cash came to perform at the prison, he surprised Sherley by singing one of the convict's own songs, "Greystone Chapel." With the help of Johnny Cash, Sherley walked out of prison a bit later as a free man with a new career.

Be persistent as you strive for a hit song. Persistence can make your dreams of becoming a successful songwriter come true.

Q. Are there many people in the industry with the ability to spot a hit song?

A. Some have a better feeling for a hit song than others. But no one really knows for sure where the next hit is coming from. Many writers have their best songs turned down by top recording executives only to have these same songs go on to become top hits. This happened with Buddy Kaye's "The Little Prince." After a three-year struggle by Kaye to arouse some interest in it, the song went on to win a Grammy award.

Q. Do you have to be very bright to create a hit song?

A. Confidence in yourself is far more important than being smart or bright. According to psychologist Eugene Raudsepp, "Millions of dollars are lost to business every year because many valuable ideas stay locked up in the minds of executives and subordinates." They don't have enough confidence to develop their ideas and get them launched. Dr. Sigmund Spaeth, a noted authority on music, once said that "the only way to write a really popular song is to put one's self first in the state of mind of a less than average person, with a less than average vocabulary, range of thought, experience and sense of grammar."

Q. For how long is a new singer put under contract by a recording company?

A. It may vary but record labels generally sign a new artist for one year.

Q. How much money should I have saved before becoming a full-time songwriter?

A. You would be wise to have enough to last you at least two years. Composer Arthur Schwartz ("Dancing in the Dark," "You and the Night and the Music") saved enough money to last two to three years. He then plunged into songwriting full time. He also found the lyricist he wanted to work with as a collaborator and wrote songs for three years, just as he had planned in advance. He then went back to his law practice but eventually gave up law and devoted full time to the music business.

Q. Would you say that a natural talent with words is a sign of a potential songwriter?

A. Songwriters who specialize in lyrics usually enjoyed working with words at some period in their younger years. A feeling for words and the rhythm expressed through them could indicate a possible lyricist, composer, or both. On the other hand, an affinity with words might not be evident until one reaches the late twenties.

Q. Should a songwriter stick to subjects he or she knows best or write about anything?

A. Generally speaking, it's better to write about the thing you know best. Everyday experiences have led to many hit songs. The case of Canadian Ruth Lowe, who wrote "I'll Never Smile Again," is worth remembering. When her husband died soon after their marriage, she was grief-stricken. She channeled her feelings into simple but most effective words and music.

Be alert to the experiences of your own life. There may be some rich material just waiting to be created. Everything that happens to you may provide the sparks for a new song.

Q. Isn't getting a hit song today mostly just good luck on the part of a songwriter?

A. Luck is being in the right place, with the right song, and at the right time. But talent, drive, and persistence are what usually produces results. Many writers claim that luck had nothing to do with their success. Rather they made it happen themselves. Songwriter, producer, and top recording executive Mike Curb backs this up: "You get the rights to a song, and the rights to an artist; you put the musicians behind the artist; you hire the arranger; and the completed product is called a master. I recorded my master, an Indian song I'd found, with a group of mine called Apache. I financed it with some of the profits of my Honda song, and sold it to Capitol."

Q. I've been trying for years to write a hit song without any success as yet. Isn't this a sign I haven't got it?

A. Cole Porter was in his late thirties before he attained any real success. Handel, the great musician, was forced to live in dire poverty when his key sponsor suddenly died. Yet, at age 60, he composed "The Messiah" and took it to Dublin, after London's top musicians sneered at it. It won wide acclaim in Dublin, carried Handel to the starry heights in no time, and was hailed as the greatest oratorio of all time.

Q. Is there any special formula in writing hit songs?

A. There's no secret or recurring formula. What works for one songwriter may not work at all for others. Hit songs have a different way of arriving and developing. Alexander Graham Bell laid down three steps for self-education that can help you in your songwriting. "Observe as many worthwhile facts as possible. Remember what has been observed. Compare the facts so as to come to conclusions. This was what made Morgan a great financier, and Napoleon a great general. It's the foundation of all education."

Superstar performer and pianist Liberace came up with a formula for success that has worked well for him.

1. "To find love, one must give love."
2. "To possess wealth, one must value wealth."
3. "To acquire health, one must live health."
4. "To experience happiness, one must express happiness."
5. "To attain success, one must positively think successfully."

This formula can be used every day of a person's life, no matter who the person is, or what his or her vocation and place in life may be.

14

The Performance Rights Question: ASCAP or BMI?

After a songwriter has one published song (one commercial record release) to his or her credit, he is eligible to join either ASCAP or BMI.

New writers sometimes get confused as to why they are urged to join one of these two organizations. There's a very good reason for joining. As pointed out earlier, one of the main sources of income for a songwriter is the performance rights royalties earned by a song from radio station use, television, live performances in nightclubs, and all other places where music is performed for a profit. Both ASCAP and BMI monitor the songs that are used on radio and television stations and charge fees for the use of ASCAP and BMI licensed songs. Both organizations collect these fees and share them with their writer-composer-publisher members.

"Moon River," the theme song of a popular film, was recorded many times by a variety of artists on single records and albums. Since then it has been played and performed an enormous number of times—on radio, on television, and live. The song has earned over a million dollars in performance rights royalties. And it will continue to earn more money as the years go by. You can see from this example that a big song's performance rights can add up to a fortune.

ASCAP and BMI Send Checks to Their Members

When you join either ASCAP or BMI, you will sign an agreement authorizing one or the other to license the right to perform your songs for profit. So naturally, the more songs you have that are being played often on radio and television stations, the more money you will receive.

Successful writers like Irving Berlin and Richard Rodgers receive much money from this performance rights source alone. Their hundreds of songs used daily for years on thousands of radio-television stations all add up to a fortune. This is a tremendous incentive to produce songs that will be popular over many years.

A writer in his twenties or thirties, after becoming a member of ASCAP or BMI, has an opportunity to establish a lifetime independent income from performance rights royalties. As he got older, Johnny Mercer used to say, "Thank God for ASCAP. The songs I wrote in my younger years are taking care of me well now." He of course went on to write many other songs to add even more to his performance rights royalties.

If you're an older writer, all the more reason to spur yourself on to create songs that will pick up a lot of performances. Royalties are an ideal way to finance retirement. The checks are sent regularly from ASCAP and BMI (ASCAP pays on a quarterly basis).

ASCAP is the older of the two organizations. All the famous songwriters of the 1920s and 1930s belonged—

Irving Berlin, Cole Porter, Rodgers and Hammerstein, Victor Herbert (active before 1920 and one of the nine founders of ASCAP, Jerome Kern, and George Gershwin. ASCAP today has a variety of modern writers on its roster. Rock, country, rhythm and blues, folk, and other music category writers are well represented. Broadcast Music Incorporated (BMI) was formed in the early 1940s.

Which One to Join—ASCAP or BMI?

ASCAP and BMI have a wide variety of writer-composer-publisher members—Broadway, rock and roll, folk song, pop, rhythm and blues, symphonic, country, and jazz.

Which licensing organization you join usually depends on the type of songwriter you are. If your main career is songwriting, then ASCAP is probably best for you. However, if you believe that you may be in songwriting for a short period of time with an occasional song that may do well, and you want your money quickly perhaps BMI would be better for you.

The amount of money you receive through ASCAP is a sum arrived at according to how long you've been a member, how popular your songs are, the overall value of your material to the total ASCAP music catalog, how many songs or musical works you're credited with, and other factors. The figure can increase year after year, according to the progress you make with your songwriting.

If you aren't a member of either ASCAP or BMI at present, set membership at the top of your list of objectives. Membership in either one is considered to be the mark of a professional. ASCAP used to require at least four published song credits. Today it's much easier to join because only one is needed. Whichever association you decide to join, stick with your decision rather than changing back and forth.

15

The Value of Contacts in the Music Centers

If there's one magic word in the music business, it is "contacts." With the right contacts, you can land straight in the ranks of money-making songwriters.

There is no substitute for getting your name known in the industry—among publishers, record label executives, A & R directors, independent record producers, artists, musicians, and writers. The value of just one or two good contacts with music publishers should be obvious to you. You have an interested outlet for your new songs. They will consider your new material, treat you fairly, then try hard to land a record deal for you on accepted songs.

How to Make Important Contacts
Here are some suggestions that have worked for a number of other writers and could work for you:

1. Do your best to attend any and all music conventions. Music conventions are a very good place to make helpful

contacts in the business. Just one key contact could lead to a major recording of one of your songs.

2.   Take notes when you read each new issue of *Billboard* and *Cash Box*. Jot down the names of people in the business that you think might be able to help you and the names of companies that seem to like and use the kind of songs you write. The addresses are often given with the names in the key music publications. Write these people short letters telling them about yourself and asking for their advice, suggestions, and assistance.

3. Even if you don't have a current record release, go to the radio stations in your area and personally meet the disc jockeys. A number of them have excellent contacts in the industry.

4. Visit the recording centers and meet people. On-the-scene writers have a big edge over the writer back home. Face-to-face meetings with people in the business are just bound to result in a few good contacts. You can imagine how many valuable contacts a New York- or Nashville-based writer develops over a period of years.

5.   Whenever you spend time in a recording center, try to obtain permission to sit in on an actual recording session. You can either write or telephone in advance to ask for permission. Some sessions are closed to visitors, while others sometimes allow a few visitors. Some writers have developed useful contacts in this way.

6. Watch the music trade publications (and your local papers as well) for the announcements of songwriting seminars that are usually held several times a year, especially in the New York, Nashville, and Memphis areas. Attend these, if at all possible. You can meet other writers, new artists, and musicians at these workshops.

7. Devise an advertisement that will call attention to yourself, your songwriting career in general, or a particular song. If the ad is attractive and unusual, you might

well receive a number of replies. You may possibly develop some useful contacts from the replies you get. Never underestimate the power of advertising. But plan your ads wisely, so they will get results.

8. One of the very best ways to make a lot of contacts is to become an announcer/DJ at a radio station. Many top names in the business today started this way, as radio disc jockeys, announcers, or news staff people. Top country singer and songwriter Bill Anderson began his career at a radio station in Decatur, Georgia.

As a radio station disc jockey you will meet record promoters, artists, musicians, songwriters, and others. How many contacts you'll be able to develop will depend on the size and importance of the station where you work.

To become a radio DJ or an announcer, you'll need at least a third-class announcer's license with broadcast endorsement. The FCC (Federal Communications Commission) gives these license tests several times a year and will send you a free booklet to study for the test. After you have your license watch the weekly ads in the back of *Broadcasting* magazine (available at most libraries). It's the main trade publication for the broadcasting industry. Positions are open for new announcers, DJ's, news people, sales talent, copywriters, and other radio industry help.

When you apply for jobs send a tape of your voice announcing records or giving the news. This audition tape can be made with a home recorder or made at a local radio station for a small fee.

9. If you live in or near a city that has one or more record companies, contact the person in charge. Let the label know that you're a local songwriter working to build a writing career. Keep your name before them. Find out who records for them and try to slant your songs for their artists.

I did this myself years ago, when I recorded one of my

own songs. The A & R director and producer of my record was Chips Moman. I was impressed with his producing ability. He had also written some hit songs himself. Chips later was a partner in the American Recording Studio where Elvis Presley cut some of his best-selling albums. Chips moved on to Atlanta for awhile and, at this writing, is in the Nashville area. Chips Moman did a lot for the growth and development of Memphis music. It was a loss for Memphis when he left for Atlanta and Nashville.

10. Dream up some dynamic publicity stunt that will immediately get your name in the newspapers. A few songwriters have used this idea with excellent results. One used a billboard to implore Perry Como to use his song. Another writer walked all the way from Texas to Nashville, in hopes of calling attention to himself.

11. Publications designed and written for songwriters list new contacts in each issue. Names and addresses are usually given. Study these lists and continually keep your own list of music contacts up-to-date.

If you are a veteran songwriter, you probably have some original ideas to add to this list. Whatever methods you use, once you establish a contact, value it through your music career.

16

Going Commercial or Writing What Pleases You

This chapter brings up an age-old question that creative songwriters have discussed, argued, and thought a great deal about through the years. Should a writer strive to create commercial material that has a chance to sell at the going rate or write whatever he or she pleases? It's a good question and one you'll need to answer sooner or later in your songwriting. Strong songs and hits have resulted from both objectives. Most serious writers, however, try to do commercial songs that will earn a lot of money for them. They need the money so that they can continue to do the work they like most—creating the songs of a nation. Some basic power in your songwriting ability may be lost or short-circuited if you try to sit down and tell yourself: "I will now write a commercial song." A song you write to please yourself may well end up also being very commercial. And one you start with the intention of making as commercial as possible may just also turn out to be a song you really like yourself.

So why not write with both goals in mind? Why not write for profit as well as pleasure? Most writers have to turn out a lot of songs each year in the hopes that at least several of them will be highly commercial and make money. Cole Porter believed in trying to write at least one new lyric every day. He did this for a number of years and composed the music for the ones he felt rated it.

So write your material with the goal of volume and the full expectation that some of your songs will be moneymakers. Don't worry about the other ones. Assume that they are simply songs you have to write on your way to your hits. Write volumes of songs, both for profit and pleasure. Your pleasure songs may end up being profitable, and I know that your profitable songs will bring you pleasure. A number of songwriters keep their good songs and throw away the rest. But writers hate to throw away songs they have written. Lines that you write on one song may help you on others.

Some writers feel strongly about writing integrity. This simply means that they try to write songs they feel. If they don't feel it, they just don't write it. If you write for awhile, you will begin to develop a writer's basic philosophy of songwriting—what you believe a song should accomplish. This gut feeling can be very helpful to you over the years. Sometimes, for example, you will know that a particular song you're writing is a hit.

The Diversity of Song Categories

The music business has become so diversified that the modern songwriter has a variety of song categories from which to choose. If you get tired of writing commercially for one music category, you have plenty of other categories to choose from. There's far more freedom today for songwriters, both in the choice of song categories and in new material itself.

Rock Songs

Rock music includes the more precise descriptions of hard rock, soft rock, country rock, epic rock, funky rock. Alice Cooper refers to one of his new albums as "pure rock and roll."

If rock songs are your interest in songwriting, you should be studying and analyzing rock songs like the many hits of the Beatles, Elton John's "Don't Go Breaking My Heart," Peter Frampton's "Baby I Love Your Way," "Devil Woman," by Cliff Richard, "I Can't Hear You No More," by Helen Reddy, "Got to Get You Into My Life," by the Beatles, and "We're an American Band," by Grand Funk Railroad. Mark Farner, lead singer of the group, backs up the strong influence that rock can have: "I've seen through experience what kind of power and effect rock has on young people. And I feel a responsibility not to lead anyone into anything bad."

The music in a rock song is the dominant part. The lyrics can sometimes add a great deal but it's basically the beat, the rhythm, the drive, and the total sound effect that reach the listener. Your songs can be styled soft rock, pure rock, hard rock, or whatever.

If you can meet any rock groups in your local area, they may be interested in using some of your rock numbers. Or form a rock group of your own. It's been done for years all over the country. It may be hard to believe, but even the Osmonds were once a new musical group. They have racked up a whopping 22 gold records, a hit television show, and they pack the crowds into the glittering palaces of Las Vegas. They are versatile and can do rock, country, or easy listening songs.

With your own musical group, you would have a perfect outlet for your new rock songs. With a rock group behind you, it's also easier to produce demos and place your songs. Record companies stay hot on the trail of rock

groups with a good sound and strong material. Having
your own group and your own material might land you a
recording contract. This is very much an era of the writer-
performer. There is a great demand for writers who can
also perform their own material. Advances on the publishing rights of the songs of a musical group can go into the
high five figures, especially if the group has been signed by
a hot record label.

Easy-Listening Music

Some records of Olivia Newton-John are a good example
of easy-listening music. As you know, songs often cross
musical borders and may show up on any number of the
charts. Come up with a song that does this and you'll
probably have a hit. "For the Good Times" is still thought
of as both a country and easy listening song. Some might
also call it MOR, or middle-of-the-road.

Easy-listening is just what it says—a softer, easier music
line. The lyrics are often more important in this type of
number than in other categories of songs. Records by Eydie
Gorme, such as "If He Walked into My Life" and "What I
Did for Love," are easy-listening. Sinatra's "Stargazer" is
easy-listening, and so is "Teach the Children," by An-
thony Newley. Many ballads and romantic love songs naturally fall into this category.

Pop Music

Pop music is more wide open today than it has ever been.
Both musical groups like the Osmonds and individual artists like Neil Diamond are going great guns in the field.
But the old way of saying I love you, need you, and can't
live without you is about gone. There's a new way of com-
municating lyric ideas in pop music. Now it's "you're
something else," "my dreams are crowded with you,"
"Lay Down Your Burden," "Afternoon Delight," and Stevie Wonder's "You Are the Sunshine of My Life."

Paul McCartney says that "when Stevie Wonder sings, he puts a little sunshine into all our lives." "Sunshine" became an almost immediate standard in the pop field. It's an excellent number to keep in mind as an example of a modern pop song. There's nothing fuzzy or complicated about the lyrics or the music. Both are simple, but they are also appealing, catchy, and can be easily hummed.

Stevie wrote his first song "Lonely Boy," when he was only ten years old. Just two years later, he had a hit song with "Fingertips." He was on his way. Unlike many songwriters, Stevie usually gets a melody first in his writing and does the lyrics a bit later.

Pop music is also the Bee Gees, Lou Rawls, Dionne Warwicke, Barry White, Walter Murphy and the Big Apple Band, Aerosmith, the Manhattans, and many more. The subject matter you can use in pop songs today is just about anything and everything you want to set to music, as long as it's done well and has basic commercial value on the market. The use of emotion is strong and direct. There's plenty of room for more songwriters to make their mark (and a million dollars as well) in the captivating world of pop music. It might be just the right field for you.

The Country Field

A lot of hit songs come out of the country field. Country music is Johnny Cash, Roy Acuff, Lynn Anderson, Loretta Lynn, Glen Campbell, Tom T. Hall, Jerry Reed, and a long roster of other stars. It's a rich field of music and is still growing.

The lyrics are very important in country songs. A big hit by Merle Haggard, "Okie from Muskogee," is a good example. The music of this song is right on the nose and adds strength. But the lyrics are the dominating part of the song. This song has earned a fortune for Haggard. The first time he sang it for troops at Ft. Bragg, the men went wild: "They were up on the bandstand, shaking my hand and hugging my neck, and they wouldn't let us sing nothing else until we did that song again."

If you want to write country songs, you can learn a lot by studying the lyrics and tune construction of some of the great country hits. Get hold of the records or sheet music of "Rose Garden," "King of the Road," "Born to Lose," "Release Me," "For the Good Times," "Rhinestone Cowboy," and Jimmy Dean's "I.O.U." Try to write country songs that will last and chalk up many record performances on radio. The years ahead look mighty good for country music. This may be the writing spot for you.

Folk Songs

Folk music has been back in demand since about the mid-1960s. Judy Collins is regarded as one of the best singers and writers in this field, although she's by no means confined to it.

Both as a writer and performer, Judy has a strong ability to project the mood of a song. In "Skyline Pigeon," by Elton John, she projects the emotion of freedom. In "Secret Gardens" she very effectively communicates the mood of change caused by the passing of time. Through this song, she's saying that a person's loved ones, people themselves as well as things, can remain young and the same in one's private memory.

If creating folk songs attracts you, listen to the recordings and songs of Judy Collins (especially the album "Bread and Roses").

Show Tunes

Show tune songwriting is a highly specialized category, but still calls for the basic ability to write songs around a given situation. Show tunes have traditionally been written according to the development, action, character motivation, and scene situations of a show's story line or plot.

But there are new and fresh approaches to show tunes today. The demand for something different has even changed the shows themselves. There's more freedom in the subject matter used for shows.

If you want to write show songs, the best place to make the contacts you'll need is New York. But there are other musical theaters in various cities where you might get a start. You can contact off-Broadway producers in hopes of landing an assignment to do some songs. If you stay with it, you'll get a foot in the door. You might try for a behind-the-scenes spot with a theater group. Stage hands, lighting and costume people, set decoration, various assistants, public relations staff, dancers, pianists, chorus people, and others are always needed.

Stephen Sondheim ("Send in the Clowns"), well-known Broadway author and composer, once said that "all he ever wanted was to make enough money from the theater to be able to write for the theater."

Other Music Branches

Other branches of music that might offer the right song category for you include gospel-sacred songs, soul, rhythm and blues, and jazz.

To find the song categories that you like best, do some experimenting. It will be unlikely that you can write commercial songs in all of the music branches. But you may be able to come up with some strong songs for several of them. You can then simply narrow it down to the one or two fields that interest you most.

17

Country Music Is Big Business

Country music. The words alone attract millions of fans, readers, musicians, and songwriters. The special sound of country music is one of the big drawing cards of the state of Tennessee.

This kind of music seems to thrive ever more with every passing year. One visit to Nashville's famed Grand Ole Opry and a ride down Record Row—with its plush recording-publishing buildings and offices—is strong proof that this down-to-earth musical art form is here to stay. Country music is big business and getting bigger all the time.

For every star who makes it in the country field, thousands fall by the wayside. Still, newcomers flock into Music City U.S.A. (Nashville's more glamorous name now), filled with hope and belief that there's a place waiting for them in the industry's coveted Hall of Fame. And there may be. New country artists and songwriters hit it big year after year.

The Guitar Is King

Many fans and would-be future greats of country music forget that some of today's illustrious names in the field started when they were very young. Chet Atkins, Glen Campbell, Johnny Cash, Eddy Arnold, and others all started playing the guitar as youngsters. No wonder they are so good today. They grew up with a new and growing art form. Like golf, great skill in country music, especially involving the guitar, takes years of work and practice. Most of the super guitar stars of today are no overnight sensations; they became professionals only after many years of practice and development.

Even the amazing Chet Atkins, with all his years of experience on the guitar, believes there is always more to learn: "I can look at a guitar and promise myself, 'I'm going to learn everything there is to know about that glorious instrument, that sacred instrument.' But nobody is ever going to learn everything about a guitar. That is what is so great about it. It will never be mastered."

Paths to Success in Country Music

How can you make it in country music? Well, there are various pathways to stardom and/or songwriting success. Some launch their own publishing or recording firms; others feel their place of glory waits among the ranks of famous songwriters. Still others think they may have what it takes for a double career of writing as well as singing. They see themselves as another Hank Williams.

The Country Music Convention

The annual Country Music Convention is held in Nashville each fall. The crowds get larger every year for this convention program saluting each new birthday of the Grand Ole Opry. Radio DJ's from across the nation pour into Nashville, along with known and unknown artists, musicians, songwriters, and recording-publishing executives. They are all fans of country music. Among their number are the possible stars of tomorrow; the singers who will become household names, the writers who will pen the gold record hit songs. Country music makes dreams come true every year. It could do the same for you.

Anyone legally connected with the music industry can attend the Country Music Convention, sponsored and supported by the Country Music Association. For a fee that is subject to increase each year, you'll be registered and will receive a book of special tickets, which must be shown before you're allowed to enter the doors to each specific program during the convention. You're also required to wear a special badge given to you at the time you register.

Back in the early 1960s, the convention was held in the old Andrew Jackson Hotel. The delegates to the convention didn't add up to such a crowd in those days. There has been a fantastic growth of interest in country music during the last ten years. News, events, and new releases in the field are followed by fans all over the world. And there are far more country music radio stations operating today.

Most of the convention program is held at the new Grand Ole Opry House (about eight miles outside of Nashville) and the downtown Municipal Auditorium. Some of the meetings begin with a meal, and the auditorium is quickly filled by the long lines of thousands of convention people who stand in line to show their passes, pick up their plate lunches, and rush to get the best seats.

The reason the crowd rushes to get the good seats is the promise of hearing stars like Bill Anderson, Sonny James, Ray Price, Lynn Anderson, Roy Clark, Porter Wagoner, and even Chet Atkins himself. If the convention crowd keeps increasing, the large city auditorium may not be big enough in the years to come.

Nashville: A New Dream Town

Nashville, Tennessee, has become in actuality another dream town, where country singers, writers, and musicians strive to become rising stars. The overall sound of country music today is slicker and more sophisticated. There are still plenty of pure country songs, but many of the numbers have a more polished sound. In fact, "uptown country" is a term used to describe smooth-sounding country songs of a romantic or big ballad nature.

WSM, the long-honored radio station, which has broadcast the Grand Ole Opry through the years, is very proud of the present Opry House and calls it "one of the unique buildings in the world."

The music is of course what attracts thousands of delegates every year to the convention. The food is fair to poor, and you stand in line for hours to get it, as well as a seat. But the crowd endures the increasing irritation of so many people, the long lines, and the growing commercialization of the festival. The reason is the appeal of the music. And some of the delegates who sit spell-bound, listening to the parade of stars, may well be up there on the stage in the years to come. It's happened many times before. "Bill Anderson started as a Georgia DJ," some of them say.

If at all possible, do your best to attend at least a few of the country music conventions. Even if you write songs in another category of music, you will find the Country Music Convention stimulating. You will see the contribution of country music to the world of music at large. You will mingle with other writers, musicians, and ambitious new artists. There's a good chance that you'll meet some of the big-name artists and recording-publishing executives. You're certain to hear a lot of commercial songs performed live by the top artists in the business.

Country music has a lot to offer you. It's exciting. It's creative. And the demand for good country songs is endless.

18

Roger Miller's Drive to Stardom

You can become a successful songwriter by developing more determination and drive. A good example of determination in action is the success story of writer-singer-performer Roger Miller. During the years when Miller was trying to get started, he wanted desperately to be a singer, but he didn't know how to go about it. He knocked around the country but couldn't get his foot in the door.

Miller hails from Erick, Oklahoma, where he had little use for school. He picked cotton to buy his own guitar—the same year he flunked out of high school.

He went to Nashville, determined to become a great country singer. "I didn't know what to do. I'd never really played before, except for gas money. At night, I'd go up to this radio station where they had an all-night DJ show, and just sit around and meet people. Anywhere there was a jam session, I'd go. And anytime anyone would lend an ear, I'd sing 'em a song."

Miller worked for Faron Young as a drummer for about a year. "I was writing and getting a few things recorded, but being a country songwriter wasn't a very lucrative thing."

He actually quit the music business three different times. He would go back home and look for a more solid job. But these jobs never lasted more than a few weeks. "I had to get back in the business. It's the only thing I could ever do."

Before he recorded "Dang Me," his first smash hit, Miller was about to move to California to try his luck as an actor. He had almost decided to give up his music career for good. He was actually in California on the day "Dang Me" came out on records. He was singing at the time in a small club in northern California. His pay was $75. In less than a week, offers started pouring in. His career soared.

Roger has no particular formula for writing hits. He wrote "Dang Me" in about five minutes. "King of the Road" took a good deal more time. "I got the words and music at the same time, but I don't know music. I can't read it. I don't even know guitar symbols—I just learned the positions on the guitar. After I've recorded a song, the publisher has someone write it out."

Today Roger Miller is riding high as a wealthy "king of the road," but not too many know the struggle he went through before finding his place in the world of music.

Roger's career really started at the Mid-South Fair in 1956. "I was a corporal then, stationed at Ft. McPherson, Georgia, in my last six months in the army. Some of the other guys and I got up this little band, the Circle A Rangers, and played in Memphis in a little booth at the fair."

Miller is versatile. In addition to singing, he plays four instruments, including the guitar, fiddle, banjo, and the drums. "I guess you could say my voice lies somewhere between Charlie Chan's and Natalie Wood's." With his smash hits, "Dang Me" and "Chug a Lug," Roger actually contributed a jazz quality to country music. Fans had never heard anything like it up to that time (1964).

Miller's television show was axed at mid-season, but he blamed himself for it: "It was just a case of too much too soon. I wasn't mature enough. I just wasn't ready for television. Television wasn't quite ready for me, either. It was too early for my kind of show."

He knows a hit song when he hears or writes one. He was the first to record Bobby Russell's "Little Green Apples." He heard about Kris Kristofferson from a friend: "Mickey Newberry put me on to Kristofferson while he was a clean-up man at one of the studios in Nashville. We got together one night and recorded 'Me and Bobby McGee' and a couple of other Kristofferson songs. Kristofferson's a giant. Mickey Newberry's great too. They're improving country music."

Helping Kristofferson was something Miller was glad to do. He had been down the road of obscurity and hard times too. To this day, when Miller visits Nashville, he remembers his days as a bellhop at the Andrew Jackson Hotel (now torn down). "Being a bellhop had more dignity than dishwashing." When he had sold some of his first songs, Roger left the Andrew Jackson Hotel. Several years later, he returned one night to the hotel and stayed in the Presidential Suite.

Be a More Determined Songwriter

Make no mistake about it: a determined person has power. No matter how much talent a person may have, he or she usually goes nowhere without enough determination. Talent without the determination to support and enforce it is like a quarterback without any blockers.

Charles Bronson worked in Pennsylvania coal mines in his early days, working a double shift for $1.00 a week. His early job career also included work as a ditchdigger, warehouse worker, apprentice bricklayer, and a baker's aide. Bronson was determined to make something of himself. Today a typical Bronson film grosses more than an incredible $70 million, with Bronson himself usually getting $20,000 a day every day he works. Asked about his huge success as an actor, his reply is straight to the point: "I look international. It's easy to identify with me."

Her special kind of determination eventually landed actress Faye Dunaway an early role on Broadway and the right movie at the right time—*Bonnie and Clyde*.

Songwriter and poet Rod McKuen credits his enormous success to those in his past who told him he couldn't do things: "They said I couldn't sing, I couldn't write books, I couldn't sell records, I couldn't sell poetry. They gave me the incentive to go out and prove them wrong."

Determination is power.

19

Other Ways of Making Money with Your Writing

In the process of trying to become a songwriter you may run out of money. This is especially true if you're spending all or most of your time and efforts on songwriting. When you need money to tide you over, here are some good part-time ways to help you finance your career.

Greeting Card Ideas

Write and sell verses to the numerous card companies in the country. There are two types of greeting cards: general and studio cards. The general cards are the four- and eight-line conventional verses you see in the stores. Many of them simply express a sincere wish or compliment to the receiver of the card. Many of these general cards look like they would be easy to write. Generally speaking, some good writing and thinking lies behind the expressed verse. Your songwriting ability will be a big help to you in doing verses for cards.

Studio cards pay better than general cards. Studio cards are those cards with the funny figures and designs on the front that lead up to a clever punch line on the inside. Studio cards are not at all like the sentimental verses you see in the general card line. Studios are usually slightly crazy and sometimes way out. The thought expressed is often a strong one, but it may get the idea over in only a few words or many.

The minimum prices paid for these humorous studio ideas are $25 and usually $50 per accepted idea. Hallmark pays $50 for crisp, sendable studio card ideas. This kind of money can add up quickly if you can sustain a continuous flow of ideas and sales. And if you offer a finished card or art (fold the paper you use into the actual size of studio cards, 4″ x 9″ dummies) for an idea, the money you are paid can be considerably higher. Happy birthday is still the most popular subject or reason for sending a greeting card. There are seasonal and other reasons for sending cards—wedding congratulations, anniversary, new baby arrivals, vacation wishes, general friendship, illness, and others. The only way to find out which subjects you can do best is to experiment with them. Writing and selling greeting card ideas is an excellent way to tide you over while you build your songwriting career.

Writing Fillers and Short Articles

Another easy way to add to your income is to write and sell fillers and short articles. The demand for such material is huge. Many magazines buy such filler material and pay good rates for it.

Fillers are used by editors to fill up the blank spaces on newspaper and magazine pages. They run from 100 words to several hundred. There are all types of fillers you can write and sell to these markets: humorous, household hints, art-of-living ideas (how you solved some personal or family problem), pet peeves, advice, religious shorts, business suggestions, and many more.

After you've written your fillers, simply type them up with your name and address in the top left corner. Send them to the editors of the many filler markets you'll often see listed in trade publications for writers. *Writer's Market,* usually published in the late fall of each year, lists thousands of markets for such fillers. By submitting many of them all the time, you stand an excellent chance of earning extra money while building your songwriting career.

Gag Lines for Cartoonists

As a songwriter, your mind thinks of new lines often. You may start a song with an appealing or unforgettable line. You could put your line-writing ability to extra use by sending original gag lines to cartoonists. If you have a good sense of humor, you should do well at this sideline.

Use 3″ x 5″ cards for these new gag lines. Describe the scene you have in mind for the cartoon in a few words. Then write the gag line itself. Work out some code number to use for each gag, so you can keep track of them. Type the code number in the upper left on the front of the card, and your name and address on the back of each card in the upper left corner.

You'll find the names and addresses of numerous cartoonists listed in each annual edition of *Writer's Market.* You can send out as many new gags as you wish. When a cartoon is sold most cartoonists pay writers either a percent of the commission or a flat fee.

The Commercial Jingle Business

The creation and sale of commercial jingles is another possible way you might pick up some extra money while trying to build your career as a songwriter. There are jingle mills located in a number of major cities in the nation.

These companies hire people to write the lyrics and music for jingles.

Jingles are also used by all types of advertisers including restaurants, auto dealers, banks, insurance companies, and all manner of firms offering a product or service to consumers.

You can easily see that songwriting ability is closely related to creating commercial jingles. If you can write a commercial song, you can probably also write a commercial jingle. It's a matter of finding out what the client wants to say in the jingle and the style of music desired. The companies that produce jingles need lyricists, composers, arrangers, musicians, and singers. You might land either a part-time (or full-time) job with one or these companies. Some jingle mills might be interested in having you do the lyrics or music for jingles, working mostly by mail on a free-lance basis. They would pay you for the material you send that they accept and can use.

Advertising agencies that are involved with getting jingles for clients may create them themselves or farm the work out to one of the established jingle companies in the country. You could check with any ad agencies in your area on the chance that they might be able to use you on either jingle lyrics, music, or both.

Teach Guitar or Piano

Still another way to earn extra money is to teach lessons on the guitar, piano, or other musical instrument. You might run a local advertisement to drum up some business, or check the music stores in your surrounding area. They might be able to use you as a music teacher.

Copywriters Earn Good Money

Many songwriters have landed good part-time and full-time positions as copywriters with advertising agencies or corporations. If you enjoy working with words, you might do very well as a copywriter. The copy you'll write will be used in print ads, radio-TV commercials, billboards, and other forms of communication.

As a copywriter, your goal is to sell the product or service. You're often called on to come up with concepts— key phrases or selling ideas—to build a campaign around.

Most copywriters are well paid for the work they do. If they produce good work, they can usually write their own tickets for the future. Some of the better copywriters have doubled their salaries with each move to another advertising agency or company advertiser. And of course you can work only part-time if you wish. When ad agencies land new accounts, they often need extra part-time help. If you're enterprising, you could even set up your own advertising copywriting service, running your company on a part-time basis, while continuing your songwriting efforts. This way you would have money coming in each month from your own clients. And with several regular clients on your roster, you could build a handy extra income, be your own boss, and still have time for your songwriting.

Keep These Related Writing Activities in Mind

Your ability to write songs is definitely related to other areas of creative writing. You may not need the extra income now, but when and if the money runs low the above suggestions could prove to be very practical while you try for your first big hit. I hope you make a million on your first smash hit. But hit songs can be elusive at times. And building a successful songwriting career also takes time and careful planning.

20

Let the All-Time Great Songwriters Inspire You

There are times in the careers of most songwriters when the going is tough. Even millionaire songwriters can sometimes feel as if the party's over. Instead of getting discouraged at such times and giving in to the temptation to throw in the towel, there's an excellent way to renew yourself with fresh inspiration. That way is to let some of the all-time great songwriters of this century inspire you.

Broadway: The Big Street

Many of the top songwriters of this century wrote for the Broadway stage. Their street of dreams was Broadway. It's the best-known street in America. It's a leading business street in the city of New York, beginning its route from the lower end of Manhattan and running out at 263rd Street. Part of it has been known and loved for years as "The Great White Way." It had and has its own special lullaby, its own style, excitement, romance, dangers, and lure. It's the big street—the street of dreams, better known as Broadway.

A hit song of the past vividly summed up the many stories Broadway could tell: "There's a Broken Heart for Every Light on Broadway." And there is. Cruise by the Great White Way, as George M. Cohan did one last time shortly before he died in the early 1940s, and the memory is filled with the glittering joy of many a past opening night. Gershwin, Romberg, Ziegfeld, Kern, Berlin, Porter, Rodgers and Hart, and Hammerstein all walked here. And their creations still linger in the wings, as if waiting for a familiar cue or another curtain call. If the present seems occasionally dismal, Broadway still has her glorious past.

Walk by the famous Palace Theater, one of about forty theaters and movie houses that belong to Times Square. Listen in the evening breeze, and you can almost hear again that great voice that got to your emotions, the voice of Judy Garland as only she could sing.

There's the Winter Garden. Flash back to the 1920s when Al Jolson came bobbing down the walkway he had built right over the audience, so he could see the faces of the people when he sang. Just the sheer mention of Broadway calls to mind the many evenings of incredible entertainment given by the great Jolson. Those who heard him in person only once never forgot him.

Broadway has become so well associated with the theater industry that various theatrical enterprises, no matter how far away from Broadway, began to be referred to as "off-Broadway." A number of plays originally launched off-Broadway eventually go to Broadway for good or ill and a chance at the bigtime. Off-Broadway can thus be a stepping-stone to theatrical success for writers, actors, dancers, composers, singers, and producers.

Irving Berlin

The career of Irving Berlin is one of the legends of the

world of music. Arriving in New York from Siberia when just a small boy, Irving got an early start in music. He wrote his first song, "Marie from Sunny Italy," as a singing waiter in Chinatown. Berlin wrote the lyrics for the song. "Alexander's Ragtime Band" was a smash hit in the early years of his career. At 21, Berlin was turning out 12 new lyrics a week.

He sold newspapers as a boy and also sang on street corners. He was fascinated with music. Over 3,000 songs have flowed from his pen through the years. Half of them have been published. And many of his published songs have been hits. "My average for hits is pretty good, I'll say that. But I've probably written more flops than anyone else too."

When the girl he loved died, Irving put his sadness into a haunting song that remains a standard to this day, "When I Lost You." He wrote many beautiful romantic ballads, but he's also written all kinds of other songs too. Some of his many hits include "Blue Skies," "Always," "Easter Parade," "How Deep Is the Ocean?" "White Christmas," and "Say It Isn't So." The songs of George M. Cohan were an inspiration to Berlin: "We all start as imitators of somebody. If you continue to imitate, then you're not a songwriter. Once you express your own talent, it's a question of how good you are."

Counting both records and sheet music, "White Christmas" has sold over 70 million copies and is listed as the all-time top seller. But of all his songs, the one Berlin likes best is "God Bless America." As he puts it, "It's the song closest to me emotionally." Berlin turned over all the royalties to the Boy Scouts and Girl Scouts of America. The song has reportedly earned a huge sum in royalties through the years.

He lost his fortune in the stock market crash of 1929, but he promptly built another with hit song after hit song.

George Gershwin once expressed his admiration for Berlin this way: "He has vitality, both rhythmic and melodic, which never seems to lose its freshness. He has that rich, colorful melodic flow—the envy of all who compose songs. His ideas are endless. His songs are exquisite cameos. Each one is as beautiful as its neighbors." Gershwin found the songs of Berlin an inspiration in his show work.

It was a great day for America when Irving Berlin arrived on our shores. His songs have touched the hearts and lives of millions of people everywhere. He will remain forever one of the immortal names of American popular music.

Jerome Kern

Jerome Kern was a composer who left the world some of its most enduring standard melodies. Kern's long list of standards include "Smoke Gets in Your Eyes," "Lovely to Look At," "The Song Is You," "Look for the Silver Lining," "They Didn't Believe Me," "All the Things You Are," and many more.

Kern was a charter member of ASCAP, founded in 1914. He composed for both motion pictures and Broadway musicals. He did the music for all the unforgettable songs of *Showboat, Roberta,* and other musicals.

Kern's music is best described as light classical. His melodies are so rich and memorable that they added depth and quality to the popular music of the 1920s and 1930s. His work certainly influenced other songwriters. Like Berlin's songs, one never tires of hearing the music of Jerome Kern. Modern musical groups continue to record their own up-tempo versions of "Smoke Gets in Your Eyes," "I Won't Dance," "All Through the Day," and other Kern favorites.

Kern once confided to friends that ever since his early youth he had always hated to go to bed at night. Why? Because he hated to spend so much wonderful time sleeping. He was afraid he would miss something. He never got over this feeling and often worked late into the night on his music.

He worked with a number of collaborators including Oscar Hammerstein, who wrote the lyrics for all of the songs from "Showboat." One of Kern and Hammerstein's most successful songs was "The Last Time I Saw Paris," which won an Oscar in 1941.

George Gershwin

George Gershwin was only 25 years old when he wrote "Rhapsody in Blue." That composition alone proved he was a genius. "Rhapsody in Blue" was a landmark in American music and quickly made a lady out of jazz, after its very successful introduction and performance by Paul Whiteman with George himself at the piano on that memorable night.

George grew up in a tough neighborhood in New York and was a friend of Edward G. Robinson, the great movie character actor. He took to music like a bird does to flying. He soon discovered that he could sit down at the piano and play almost any tune he had heard.

He knew while still in his teens that he had to be in the music business. He quit high school to take his first job in the business as a pianist. He later left Tin Pan Alley to study music and write show songs.

His brother, Ira, had a talent with lyrics from an early age, and the two brothers found that they worked well as song collaborators.

George was driven in his career. Music quickly became his life. He never married, though reports stated that he had proposed to a well-known actress. He instinctively seemed to know who the right singers were for his songs. There's no telling how far he would've gone in music had he lived beyond 38 years. His "Concerto in F," "An American in Paris," and "Porgy and Bess" give strong hints of the evolvement of his music.

The music and songs of George Gershwin strongly reflect the time in which he lived. Such gems as "Embraceable You," "I Got Rhythm," "But Not for Me," "The Man I Love," "Someone to Watch Over Me," and so many others are all evidence that the music he left is still magical. There'll never be another like him.

William C. Handy

Handy's father was a minister and thought little of musicians. So young Handy had to finally leave home to follow his music goal. Working his way to Birmingham, Alabama, he taught school for two years. When the Panic of 1893 hit, he went to the Chicago World's Fair as leader of a quartet he had organized. The quartet was not warmly received and he was promptly fired.

For the next several years, Handy worked as bricklayer, music teacher, traveling band leader, and solo cornetist for a minstrel show. He finally formed his own band and began to move closer to his dreams.

While at a dance in Mississippi, Handy noted the great enthusiasm with which people responded to a band composed of bass violin, mandolin, and guitar. It reminded him of the music he had listened to in his youth— traveling bands in barber shops and spirituals in his father's Methodist church. The people seemed to love this kind of music and their reaction made Handy realize that this southern music would be popular elsewhere. It was then that he made an important move to Memphis, Tennessee.

Soon after arriving in Memphis, he began collecting and writing down his experiments with the type of songs he had heard all over. He started to compose, and one day on Beale Street the "blues" were born. Crude forms of the blues date back to 1870. George Gershwin once acknowledged that Handy's "St. Louis Blues" influenced his own writing of "Rhapsody in Blue" and "Porgy and Bess."

Using a basic blues tune, Handy wrote a campaign song for a local candidate named Ed Crump. Crump was elected and Handy's career was on its way. It wasn't long before he headed a chain of bands that sent out up to 90 men in a single night. Handy changed the campaign song and renamed it "Memphis Blues." Determined to see it published, he printed a thousand copies on his own and began to increase his composing work with more than 60 numbers flowing from his pen over a 20-year period.

He next formed a partnership with Harry Pace, a songwriter, and established a music publishing company in New York. This action began the great change in Tin Pan Alley that had no equal until the arrival of ragtime.

Handy was 40 years old when he wrote his famous "St. Louis Blues," which catapulted him into fame and fortune. Published in 1914, it became one of the most popular hits in Tin Pan Alley history. Many years after its writing, it was said to have still brought in as much as $25,000 a year in royalties.

He didn't limit himself to the blues. He wrote secular songs, spiritual arrangements, and worked both as orchestra leader and composer. In 1925, leading his own 30-piece band and a large chorus, he made his first Carnegie Hall concert appearance, tracing music from African beginnings to spirituals and jazz.

Some have said that Handy was destined to become a famed composer. Without his great love for music, a persistent desire to make his dream a reality, and a continual striving to become a professional musician, it's doubtful that he would have hit the heights he did.

It's been written that "genius is one percent talent and 99 percent work." Handy had a reservoir of talent, but more important, he had the drive and persistence to back that talent and make his dream come true. Few knew that the last 15 years of his life were spent in total blindness. He had others write down his tunes and melodies. He lives on in the music he left us.

Cole Porter

Cole Porter was an Indiana boy. He came from a wealthy family and graduated from Yale. One semester of law school at Harvard was all he could take. He switched to the Harvard Music School and studied for two years.

After more music study in Paris, Porter tried to score with his first musical, *See America First*. It failed. Frustrated, he joined the French Foreign Legion. But a portable piano strapped across his back went with him, and he played the favorite songs of the soldiers.

He later gained quite a reputation as a playboy by throwing lavish champagne parties in Paris and in Venice. Most producers wouldn't take him seriously. His first show successes (score and lyrics) were *Kitchy Koo* and *Greenwich Village Follies*. One song, "An Old-fashioned Garden," was a big success.

While in Venice, Porter met Ray Goetz, who needed a composer for a new show he was producing called *Paris*. Porter got the job, and his career began to move. He did the score and lyrics for *Anything Goes,* and it was a huge hit.

Cole Porter is a perfect example of the belief that a songwriter doesn't have to sweat and strain to turn out good songs. He got many of his best ideas and inspiration while at play. He thrived on entertainment, and it helped him produce effective work. He loved parties and planned his daily schedule around having a good time. Three and four parties a night were a regular routine. He never went to bed until sun-up, and worked from 11 A.M. to about 5 P.M.

When he was 46, Porter was thrown from a horse, fracturing both legs, while riding at a Long Island club. He endured many operations on his legs in the years that followed and eventually had to have one amputated near the end of his life.

But even the accident didn't stop Cole. He wrote his music and lyrics in bed when necessary. His song credit list—music and lyrics—include "Night and Day," "I've Got You Under My Skin," "In the Still of the Night," "Rosalie," "I Get a Kick Out of You," "Wunderbar," "Easy to Love," "Begin the Beguine," and lots of other well-loved songs. His favorite subject for songs was love.

Porter once revealed the source of the lyric idea for "Night and Day." As he had dinner with Mrs. Vincent Astor one night, she became irritated by the sound of a broken eaves spout and let Porter know it by exclaiming: "That drip drip drip is driving me mad."

Porter admitted that he was dedicated to avoiding boredom: "I'm spending my life escaping boredom, not because I am bored, but because I don't want to be. I'm engaged in the business of entertaining myself, which enables me to entertain, as much I can, the world."

Richard Rodgers

Richard Rodgers has earned an honored place among the all-time great songwriters of the twentieth century. In his chief collaborations with ace lyricists Lorenz Hart and Oscar Hammerstein, Rodgers created hundreds of songs that are still played and heard today on radio, television, and records.

Just a few of the song jewels composed by Rodgers include "Manhattan," "Ten Cents a Dance," "The Blue Room," "You Took Advantage of Me," "Isn't It Romantic," "Blue Moon," "My Romance," "There's a Small Hotel," "Where or When," "It Might as Well Be Spring," and a long list of others.

A number of the most memorable Broadway musicals were composed by Rodgers and either Hart or Hammerstein. If Rodgers had only done the music for *Oklahoma, South Pacific,* and *The Sound of Music* alone, he would still rate a top place among the great songwriters. But he did many other shows too, including *State Fair, Carousel, Pal Joey, The Boys From Syracuse, On Your Toes, Allegro, Do I Hear a Waltz?* and more.

He made his affection for the love song very clear in an article he wrote a few years ago: "A great variety of emotions can be expressed through a love song. A girl may be described as 'Younger Than Springtime,' or serenaded 'With a Song in My Heart,' or hailed as 'The Most Beautiful Girl in the World'."

According to Rodgers, "A love song doesn't even have to be about a human being. It's been known to express affection for a blue room, a small hotel, the sound of music, and all kinds of favorite things. The phenomenon of a person convinced that he has known and loved someone before, even though they're meeting for the first time, was the theme of 'Where or When'."

Another Rodgers song, "Do I Love You Because You're Beautiful?" took up the age-old question of whether beauty induces love or love induces beauty.

In his book, *The Rodgers and Hammerstein Story*, Stanley Green quotes Mr. Rodgers on song collaboration: "A good collaboration is one where minds, emotions, and intellects meet." Rodgers certainly had two outstanding collaborators in Lorenz Hart and Oscar Hammerstein. Throughout the many years of collaboration with them he never had an argument with either lyricist. Our world is a far better one because of the sound of the music of Richard Rodgers. Even his name has a musical ring to it.

George M. Cohan

Although he claimed he was born on the fourth of July (the records say July third), the rip-roaring patriotic zeal of many of his songs reflect it. A statue of Cohan stands in the heart of Times Square in New York and seems a fitting place for the man who owned Broadway.

Cohan was a showman through and through. A child performer with his parents and sister, "The Four Cohans" were one of the most popular acts of the vaudeville circuit. They danced. They sang. And George soon supplied them with new songs and eventually with George M. Cohan produced shows.

Cohan did everything. He wrote, acted, danced with an electrifying style all his own (James Cagney won an Oscar portraying him on the screen), sang, directed, and produced his own shows as well as other touring shows in partnership with his friend Sam Harris. He once spent $4,000 producing a show he made $1 million on.

He had only six weeks of formal school in his life. He literally grew up in theaters traveling with his parents from theater to theater and town to town. But after he grew up, New York City and Broadway were his main beat.

George M. wrote over 500 songs including such hits as "Give My Regards to Broadway," "Yankee Doodle Dandy," "Harrigan," "You're a Grand Old Flag," "Forty-five Minutes From Broadway," and many others. Cohan was the first songwriter to receive a Congressional Medal of Honor for a song. The medal was given to him by Franklin Roosevelt for his song that lifted the hearts of America's fighting men in both World War I and World War II. The song was "Over There." It still sounds as good today as the day he wrote it.

George M. was a yankee doodle dandy who captured the

heart of America. The world won't forget he was here.

Sammy Cahn and James Van Heusen

Back in my college days, I used to marvel at the continuous string of hit songs turned out by one of the most successful songwriting teams of them all, Sammy Cahn and Jimmy Van Heusen.

It seemed to me that whenever a new song won me over with both music and lyrics, that song invariably turned out to be a Cahn-Van Heusen tune. I figured the two had to have some secret of churning out so many hits. They did. It was called talent.

Both of them have worked with other collaborators, but their most successful songs have been cowritten with each other. Their credits include "All the Way" (still one of the best ballads ever written), "Call Me Irresponsible," "High Hopes," "Where Love Has Gone," "The Second Time Around," and "The Tender Trap."

Van Heusen went to New York in the early 1930s with over 500 songs to market. But publishers wouldn't take his material. So he took a job running a freight elevator at a New York hotel and wrote songs whenever he could. After the hotel played one of his songs, a music publisher took the song and hired Van Heusen as a staff pianist. He met Jimmy Dorsey in the late 1930s and wrote music for his lyrics. The song, "It's the Dreamer in Me," sold 90,000 copies. Van Heusen was on his way.

Sammy Cahn is a very active writer. He has the uncanny ability to write many good lyrics in only one day. While holding down a job to support himself, Cahn devoted all his spare time to songwriting. Publishers generally paid little attention to him in those early days. He began doing special material for various band acts, comedians, and singers. He even rented office space in the offices of a major booking agent to have the appearance of being a professional. This way he got to meet a number of comedians and singers. They used some of his songs, and he was on his way to a fabulous career.

Sammy Cahn, like few other songwriters, is doubly blessed with an ability to demonstrate a song. He can sing and perform his own songs well. This has helped him to place songs with a number of VIP star names. He usually starts a song from a title and a key line or phrase evolves from there.

Hank Williams

The reason that country music became a new popular art form can be summed up in two words: Hank Williams. No roster of great writers is complete without his name.

Hank was a very inventive songwriter. His lyrics tell about a real world and are saturated with honesty and reality. "Move It on Over" paints the picture of a man who comes home late and discovers that his wife has locked him out. So he crawls into the doghouse, muttering the title line to the dog.

Williams believed that lyrics are very important. At least he gave the lyrics in his own songs more attention than the music. He felt that once he got the words of a song to his liking, the music would usually take care of itself. A study of his lyrics reveals that they dominate his songs; the lyrics seem to stand out more than the music.

He was a strong believer in simplicity: "If you're gonna sing a song, sing 'em somethin' they can understand." He practiced what he preached.

For all the success he attained, those who knew Hank have described him as a lonely man. But he helped pave the way for the remarkable development of country music as an important branch of the music world. And he did it with songs like "Your Cheatin' Heart," "Cold Cold Heart," and "A Mansion on the Hill."

Great Songwriters Can Always Inspire You

As you've probably realized, the great writers covered in this chapter had similarities in their songwriting careers. Being aware of them can give you guidance and inspiration in your own songwriting efforts.

1. They were completely dedicated to songwriting. Music was their life.

2. A number of them did their best work in collaboration with a cowriter.

3. Some had a great deal of music training before launching their careers.

4. None of them got discouraged and quit writing songs when their songs were rejected.

5. All of them believed there was a place for them in music.

6. Some of them developed their new songs from a mere title or key phrase.

7. Most of them were prolific songwriters (over 3,000 songs by Irving Berlin alone).

8. Most of them revealed an early interest and/or ability in music.

9. Five of them wrote complete songs (both lyrics and music).

10. All of the songwriters wrote songs that have become standards through the years.

Whenever you are discouraged over the progress of your own songwriting career, remember some of these all-time great writers. Remember how Cole Porter kept writing from a hospital bed. Handy struggled many years before he found his place in music; George Gershwin had such a short time to create his music. Better yet, listen to their songs, to the utter simplicity of the lyrics, the strong ideas behind their songs, and the way the music and lyrics all come together.

21

Writers of the Modern Era

Most people agree that the modern era of songwriting and music began with the explosion of Elvis Presley on the musical scene in the mid-fifties. Certainly by 1960, the modern era was off and running.

Some of the writers included in this chapter may also fall within your own selection of all-time great writers, and certainly the list here is far from complete.

I believe the late Johnny Mercer's collaboration on songs with Henry Mancini belongs in the classification of modern era writers.

Mancini-Mercer

The Henry Mancini-Johnny Mercer team got started in the early 1960s with an enormous hit standard called "Moon River." The song was from the hit film, "Breakfast at Tiffany's." Mercer considered "Moon River" to be one of his best lyrics. Johnny originally planned to title "Moon

River" "Red River." The problem was that there was already an existing song about Red River. So he changed the title to "Blue River." Unsatisfied, he switched to "June River" and finally to "Moon River."

Some of Mercer's earlier hits include "Accentuate the Positive," "Jeepers Creepers," "I Wanna Be Around" (the idea and several lines were sent to him by a woman in Youngstown, Ohio), and "Dream." He got an Oscar for "On the Atchinson, Topeka and the Santa Fe." Of his own songs, the ones he liked best were "Laura," "That Old Black Magic," and "Dream." He received four Oscars in all.

The title for "Accentuate the Positive" was given to him: "That title was told to me by a guy who'd heard it in a Father Divine sermon. Three or four or fifteen years later I used it as a title. Harold Arlen liked it. We put it in a movie, and it got pretty big. I never heard from the guy who told it to me or from Father Divine either."

With the strong composing talents of Henry Mancini, Johnny Mercer wrote some of his best songs. Mancini had of course already built a very successful career for himself as a composer, conductor, arranger, and pianist. He did the musical scores for many top films and television shows of the 1950s and 1960s ("Peter Gunn," and "Mr. Lucky," for example). The two writers created two Oscar-winning songs in "Moon River" and "Days of Wine and Roses." Some of their other memorable songs are "Moment to Moment," and "The Sweetheart Tree."

While they didn't work together for very long, their names are associated and remembered as a team. Some of the very best songs of the 1960s were theirs.

Henry Mancini is still creating excellent music. But the loss of Johnny Mercer saddened many people in the industry, as well as those who knew and loved his songs. He went a long way from his early days in Savannah, Georgia. He'll be long remembered as a giant figure in the world of songwriting.

Burt Bacharach and Hal David

Lyricist Hal David wrote many songs before he teamed up with composer Burt Bacharach, but his greatest success has come in collaboration with Burt. The dynamic duo have turned out instantly recognized hits like "Raindrops Keep Fallin' on My Head," "What the World Needs Now Is Love," "Alfie," "Wives and Lovers," "What's New, Pussycat?" "Walk On By," "A House Is Not a Home," "Promise Her Anything," "The Windows of the World," and a string of others.

Dionne Warwicke has recorded many of their songs and feels that a lot of their material is right for her. "They don't write especially for me. It just feels that way. When I do something of theirs, it becomes mine. I make it mine. I know what they're trying to say and what they are saying."

Because today's songwriter is more free, David believes that the good songs of today are often more inventive than the material of a generation ago. "We all learn from the past: what is good remains, what is bad is forgotten. The trash of today is no worse than the trash of yesterday. Perhaps today's trash may be a little noisier; that's a result of our electronic age, not of the songwriter." Bacharach and David won an Oscar for their very popular hit "Raindrops," from the enormously successful film, *Butch Cassidy and the Sundance Kid.* This song is a good example of the ingredients of a Hal David-Burt Bacharach hit: simplicity, emotional appeal and impact, believability, and a catchy tune that makes you start humming without even realizing it. *What the world needs now* is more Bacharach and David songs.

Paul Anka

It seems as if everything Paul Anka writes turns out to be a huge hit. Paul has mastered the art and craft of picking a strong theme for a song, gripping the listener's attention from the very opening line, and sustaining that close attention and interest all the way through to the last note.

Partly in preparation for this chapter and because I've long admired Anka's work as a songwriter and artist, I caught one of his midnight shows last June at Caesar's Palace in Las Vegas. Paul appears in Vegas regularly and in the top nightclubs all over the country. He was all over the stage. He led the orchestra, played the piano, came out into the audience and serenaded the young ladies in the crowd, and, best of all, traced his own musical career, singing the hits he has created over the last 20 years.

Paul Anka has an amazing ability to get emotional appeal into his lyrics and give them just the right music. In Las Vegas I had a feeling that no other music but his own would be right for a Paul Anka lyric. Songs like "Let Me Try Again," "Havin' My Baby," and the always powerful "My Way" are hard to forget. I personally think that "My Way" alone would rank Paul Anka as one of the best songwriters of the modern era. It's a fine example of all that a song standard should be.

He sang a medley of some of his early hits: "Diana," "Lonely Boy," and "Put Your Head on My Shoulder." Near the end of his act, he sang a moving rendition of the song "Feelings" and then introduced the writer of that song who was present in the audience that night. At the end of the show, Paul got a standing ovation from the audience. Two young ladies who had come all the way from Pennsylvania to hear Anka and see his show also had been there the night before for the same midnight Anka show. As they put it, "It's well worth paying our money twice to hear him sing. We'd like to come back tomorrow night." Maybe they did. This is the typical reaction Paul receives from his fans.

He knows how to put it all together: lyrics, music, arrangements, and superior song styling and performance. He's as dynamic as a modern Al Jolson. Every songwriter should hear him in person because of his remarkable ability to not only write excellent songs but also put them over in a highly professional way. Seeing and hearing him perform made me realize how few songwriters there are who have the ability to write very strong songs and to also sing them well too. Paul Anka does it all.

Keith Carradine

Keith is a son of the famous character actor John Carradine. He launched his music career by playing piano and guitar in high school. From there, he landed a part in the New York stage production of *Hair*.

After appearing in several Robert Altman movies, Carradine happened to play a few of his songs for a group of people at Altman's home. Altman heard "I'm Easy" and liked it so well that he used the song in his *Nashville* film. Carradine sang two of his own numbers in *Nashville*. "I'm Easy," won the Academy Award for best film song. Carradine is another strong blending of artist, writer, musician, and actor. Other films he's been seen in include *Thieves Like Us* and *McCabe and Mrs. Miller*.

It looks as if Keith may divide his time between acting and music projects. He is very interested in both. With an Oscar and several film acting credits already to his name, Keith Carradine has a great future ahead of him.

Bill Anderson

Back when country music singer-composer Bill Anderson was starting his career, country songs were called hillbilly music. "The songs were very basic, with three-note progressions. Lyrically they left a lot to be desired. They were very crude in those respects."

Country music has developed quite a bit since that time, and Bill Anderson has made a major contribution to the industry. One of its most respected and talented stars, Anderson is another one of those rare total performers: writer, composer, artist, and musician. He also is seen regularly on television.

Bill has a degree in journalism from the University of Georgia and got his start in the business as a disc jockey on a country radio station. His string of hit songs has been continuous. Naturally he turns out more hit songs in those years when he's not touring the country so much and has more time for songwriting.

Just a few of his many hits include "City Lights," "Still," "Quits," "Slippin' Away," "If You Can Live With It," "The Lord Knows I'm Drinkin'," and "Mercy."

Bill's advice on songwriting is valuable and right on target for all types of writers: "A writer must have time to think. To create, his mind must be relaxed. When there are things bugging me, I can't write. Yet I think all writers run into periods when they write hot and cold. Moods of depression never last. I think anyone capable of writing once is always capable of writing."

Bobby Lord, in his book *Hit the Glory Road*, quotes Anderson on the greatest asset of a songwriter. According to Bill, "It's not his vocabulary, not his musical knowledge, but a quality expressed by a word I have never seen used in connection with songwriting: empathy. He must be able to identify with people and put himself in their place."

Anderson believes the future will bring an even larger audience for country music: "Young people are coming to the concerts, listening to the radio and buying the records, either because they dig them or just out of curiosity. Country music deals with basics—things they can understand and feelings they can trust. I think our music fits with the mood of the country and of the times." As long as there are writers and artists around of Bill Anderson's caliber, country music does have a fabulous future.

Paul Williams

Paul Williams is one of the best new writers to come along in the entire era of modern-day songwriting. He's a frequent guest on the "Tonight Show" and appears regularly in Las Vegas, in concerts, and in nightclubs, He often hosts award-winning programs in the industry.

Paul has made a successful name for himself with such outstanding hit songs as "I Won't Last a Day Without You," "Never Had It So Good," "You and Me Against the World," and "Let Me Be the One." He comes across well in performing his own songs. His voice is unusual and the emotional impact of the lyric and central idea behind his songs are well communicated by his singing style.

Paul believes that many potentially good songwriters don't stick with their writing because they feel as if the odds are too great against coming up with a blockbuster hit. Paul says this is far from the truth. Writers can still make good money without having a monster hit. "One piece of advice I always give to a budding songwriter is to try to develop songs that will endure, songs that can be performed and recorded by many artists, that will be played through the years and programmed consistently on radio and television, in concerts and nightclubs."

Paul feels that it's too bad so many talented newcomers to songwriting get discouraged. The success that can be achieved in the field is tremendous. "The kind of money that a successful songwriter can make is mind-boggling. He makes royalties on performances of his songs in every possible medium. And songwriters should have even more money coming their way when jukeboxes in the nation start paying a royalty (as expected through the new copyright law) on the recorded songs that are played." Paul confirms the fact that you don't have to be a superstar writer to make good money in the music business. The top writers receive royalties estimated in the six figures. But according to Williams, "There are about 1,000 writers today earning between $20,000 to $25,000 a year; 6,000 writers pulling in between $10,000 to $15,000 in royalties annually."

If newer writers didn't get discouraged when they don't get an enormous hit that coasts up and down the charts, the number of songwriters earning this kind of money could double.

Paul advises songwriters to "be aware of the craftsmanship of a song and try to build in structure. A commercial song must also be universal, with an appeal to a wide variety of people."

One of Paul's proudest accomplishments was the clever song material and scoring (lyrics and music) he did for the film *Bugsy Malone*. The film was unusual and built on a new idea: the entire cast was made up of children. Paul wrote the title song from the film and performed it a number of times on nationwide television.

There seems little doubt that Paul Williams will continue to be one of the top songwriter-performers for some time to come. Many future hits will bear his name and the stamp of his personality and performing style.

Elton John and Bernie Taupin

Songwriter and artist Elton John has an almost unbelievable effect on audiences. At the end of one of his concerts in New York's Madison Square Garden, at least 20,000 people cheered, stamped, and even sang along with Elton. The floor of the Garden was shaking as if a fresh earthquake had just hit town. This is the kind of overwhelming effect that Elton John can have on an audience.

Bernie Taupin writes the lyrics for Elton and usually settles on a title before developing the lyric. "Before I start the song, I'll think of something that I like the sound of and work from there. Then sometimes I'll get a line or something that I particularly like, and I'll work around that. It's usually a title or a certain line."

Taupin met Elton John in 1968 after entering a music talent contest in London. The two have worked successfully together ever since. The songs they have turned out have made Elton John a multimillionaire, and his annual income continues to run into the millions.

Taupin gives the lyrics to Elton as soon as they're written. "I just give them to Elton and he starts work on them." Taupin, an Englishman, follows no set pattern for the lyrics. The number of stanzas usually varies from song to song.

Elton and Bernie have turned out such hits as "Crocodile Rock," "Don't Let the Sun Go Down on Me," "Daniel," and "Elderberry Wine." Elton has done the music for all of Taupin's lyrics. For "The One Who Writes the Words," it must be nice to have some sure fire Elton John music that you know is going to skyrocket a new song on its way. Their collaboration spells rock hit after hit. And then some.

Kris Kristofferson

Another big-name writer of today's era is Kris Kristofferson. Like Roger Miller, Kristofferson found success only after years of struggle and dedication to his writing.

He turned down jobs that he felt would take all of his time. He refused to quit writing and always made sure he had the necessary time to spend on his songwriting.

The late 1960s in Nashville were tough years for him. He worked as a common laborer, digging ditches, and was also a bartender in Nashville's Record Row area. He eventually landed a clean-up job at a Nashville recording studio, earning $58 a week.

The quality that stands out in his songs perhaps more than any other is simplicity; his lyrics provide examples of the contemporary way of expressing emotion. All trite and overused lines are out. "For the Good Times" was a fresh way of creating an emotional effect. And he did it with simple words.

Like Keith Carradine, Kristofferson has shown acting talent, most notably in the film *The Sailor Who Fell from Grace with the Sea*. As another actor, songwriter, recording artist, and musician, Kris should have a lot to contribute in the years ahead. His friend Roger Miller calls him a giant in the business.

Marvin Hamlisch

Marvin Hamlisch is the young New York composer who has been carting off all kinds of song awards in recent years. He won an incredible three Oscars and an Oscar nomination on the same night for his work in *The Sting* and *The Way We Were*.

Marvin grew up in New York City and wrote his first hit at 17 for singer Lesley Gore ("Sunshine, Lollipops and Rainbows"). He frequently appears as a guest, or guest host on the "Tonight Show" and always treats the audience to a number or two on the piano.

Marvin, who has already accomplished more than many songwriters do in an entire lifetime, seems blessed with a rare gift of rich melodic invention. His song, "The Way We Were," will be a standard for many years to come. He can easily write for both the Broadway stage and motion pictures, and I predict that some of the top song hits of tomorrow will be Marvin Hamlisch numbers.

Stevie Wonder

Blind from birth, Stevie Wonder started making his dream of a music career come true at an early age. By the time he was eight, he could already play several instruments, including the harmonica, drums, and the piano. From the day he first set foot in the Motown recording studios, he knew he had found his future.

The Motown staff called him the "little boy wonder." He was there every day after school and literally grew up in the recording studios of Motown.

As he got older, Stevie studied classical music at the Michigan School for the Blind. But he remained close to all his friends at Motown. Some of his early hits in those days were "Uptight," "For Once in My Life," and "I Was Made to Love Her."

When Stevie turned 21 he collected about one million dollars—money that had been held in trust for him by the founder of Motown Records. At this same time he had already sold a whopping 30 million records.

His albums are big sellers, as are his single records. In his apartment in New York or his home in Los Angeles, he continues to write and sing exactly what he feels. His pop appeal is universal, and his records sell everywhere.

Stevie believes that a songwriter has cycles. "Certain weeks you can write and then the next week you can't do nothing. It's an involuntary movement. But you can't be getting worried when it doesn't come." Many more hits are expected from Stevie, who seems to be well tuned-in to the rhythms of the world.

The Beatles

The world-famous, incomparable Beatles may have broken up, but their legend continues. There always are recurring rumors that the four idols may get together again for a series of new appearances or another American tour, and whenever such rumors start flying, all hell breaks loose and the telephone switchboards are tied up for hours.

No list of songwriters of the modern era would be complete, of course, without the Beatles. The songs by Lennon and McCartney represent much of the pure gold from the hits of the 1960s, better known as the decade of the Beatles.

Love songs were one of their specialties. "Wait," a song about coming home, was a transition song in their development. "I'll Follow the Sun" (1964) revealed Paul McCartney's developing compassion and tenderness as a songwriter.

"Yesterday" (1965), one of their most beautiful and haunting songs, is a perfect example of the timeless quality so many songwriters strive to get into their material. The song can be performed today, or in the year 2,000 with no loss of dynamic effect because you never tire of hearing the lyrics or the melody. Again, as in many Beatle songs, the subject is universal—the loss of love.

The Beatles crammed the 1960s with solid gold hits— "Michelle," "I'm Only Sleeping," "Good Day Sunshine," "Eleanor Rigby," "Sexy Sadie," "Penny Lane," "Julia," "The Fool on the Hill," "Tomorrow Never Knows," "I Don't Wanna Be a Soldier," "How," and many others.

Many feel that the Beatles were the top writers of this century. Certainly they were the top musical group that wrote and performed their own material. But few expected that. John Lennon's aunt told him once that the guitar was all right "but you'll never earn your living with it." John gave her a plaque with those very words on it to hang over her fireplace. Still, who could have predicted the musical throne for them?

John Lennon and Paul McCartney were reported to have written 150 songs before they recorded their first number, and of course many veteran songwriters insist that is as it should be. Perhaps the Beatles serve as an example of the possibility that formal music study may kill or stifle the natural talents of at least some songwriters. All you need is musical charisma and amazing talent.

22

Paul Francis Webster: Lyric Man Extraordinary

One of America's most talented and successful lyricists, Paul Francis Webster, has specialized in songs featured in major films. When we talked, he had been nominated 15 times for the coveted Academy Award and had won the Oscar three times for the best song from a motion picture.

Paul Francis Webster has written a thousand songs—538 of them published. Over a hundred of them are unforgettable motion picture songs, instantly recognized and loved by people everywhere. His three Oscars to date were for "Love Is a Many-Splendored Thing," "Secret Love," and "The Shadow of Your Smile." He has also received Grammies, as well as special prizes, gold medals, and other awards from music trade publications and film critics. The walls of his study are lined with gold records and trophies.

Webster has collaborated with many of the greatest light-music composers of modern times. His lyrics have blended with the music of Sammy Fain, Hoagy Carmichael, Duke Ellington, Andre Previn, Sigmund Romberg, Dmitri Tiomkin, Rudolph Friml, and many other well-known names. The songs resulting from these collaborations remain all-time favorites because of their perfect blend of words and music.

A Strange Beginning Launched His Remarkable Career

In 1930, at a Friday night basketball game and dance at Woodmere Academy on Long Island, Johnny Loeb, a cousin of the murdered Bobbie Franks (the victim of the infamous Leopold-Loeb Case) asked his friend, Webster, if he had ever written a song. Surprised at the question, Webster said that he hadn't and knew nothing about songwriting. But the question got the two of them thinking.

After the dance that night, on a used piano above the school gym, Webster and Loeb wrote a song. It was a waltz called "Masquerade." Webster remembers that night as if it were yesterday: "The light had been shut off, so we used a cigarette lighter while creating and writing the song."

This somewhat strange beginning was Webster's first attempt at songwriting. That night changed his entire life. "I might never have started writing songs," he told me, "if my friend Loeb hadn't asked me that question." Because of the events of that memorable night and the remarkably successful career that followed, Paul Francis Webster is convinced to this day that he was destined to become a songwriter.

His First Song—a Hit

"Masquerade" broke some of the rules of traditional songwriting. It had 64 bars instead of the usual 32. It also had too wide a range. But for someone who had never written a song before, it was incredibly good and showed the promise of a real writing career.

"Masquerade" and other songs from his pen taught Webster that a writer shouldn't worry if some of his songs don't follow the rules: "The marriage of words and music is an abstract and highly subjective science (sometimes an art) and cannot be imprisoned in a cage of iron-clad rules. Exceptions are always breaking through the aforementioned cage to confront and confound the rules-makers."

But as every songwriter knows, writing a song and selling it are two different things. "Masquerade" was turned down by every publisher in New York. Convinced the song had something, Webster took a train to Chicago to see Paul Whiteman at the Edgewater Beach Hotel. It took three nights of waiting before he finally got a chance to talk Whiteman into listening to "Masquerade."

Whiteman thought the song was interesting and said he would introduce it the following month in New York. A symphonic arrangement was done, and the song was published by Leo Feist. "Masquerade" earned $12,000 for each of its two creators. For two youths just in their early twenties, it was a bonanza, especially in 1930.

Webster's Career Skyrockets

And more success was on the way. He joined the American Society of Composers, Authors, and Publishers (ASCAP) in 1932. Just two years later, Webster and Lew Pollack had the number one song in the country, "Two Cigarettes in the Dark," still a favorite with millions of Americans. With the success of this top song, Webster was soon offered $300 a week to move to Hollywood to write songs for the very popular Shirley Temple films. He made the move to the coast, worked for Fox Films, and stayed. This led to many other motion picture assignments through the years. Webster is today credited as the lyric writer of songs featured in over 100 film and stage productions.

Experiences Can Help a Songwriter

Two of Webster's favorite cities are Hong Kong and Florence, Italy. A windswept hilltop scene he remembered in his travels, as a boy of nineteen, inspired him to write one of his best known songs, "Love Is a Many-Splendored Thing." The song came as a result of a film assignment originally called "A Many-Splendored Thing." Webster felt that the film and its title would be improved by adding the words "Love Is" before "A Many-Splendored Thing." His suggestion of course was followed.

Songwriters sometimes get strong feelings about their work. Some of them instinctively know when they've written a song that can go all the way, given a fair chance. After he had finished "Love Is a Many-Splendored Thing," Webster realized that the song could become a great standard of lasting value. But he was sure the song needed a fine demonstration recording to give it the best chance it deserved. So Webster, with a studio orchestra recording of his song, was confident that "Love Is a Many-Splendored Thing" would interest the record labels and key recording artists.

It didn't. Incredible as it may sound, the song was turned down by all the top record companies. Catching his second wind, Webster took the song to his friend and next-door neighbor—that bundle of charm, energy, and talent known as Doris Day. She didn't like the song either. A copy of the demo recording was flown to singer Tony Martin, who was then appearing in Las Vegas. He also turned the song down!

Webster was beginning to wonder if he was wrong about the song. Still, he refused to give up on it. Three more name recording stars said no, including Eddie Fisher and Nat King Cole. Five major artists rejected the song, four of them within a three-month period.

But Webster's belief in the song and refusal to quit were

finally rewarded. The demonstration recording of the song was played for the Four Aces, and this musical group liked what they heard. They quickly recorded "Love Is a Many-Splendored Thing," which became a tremendous national hit for them.

Since then, the song has been recorded hundreds of times by well-known recording artists, vocal groups, and musicians. It has become a giant standard, played and performed in nightclubs and on radio and television year after year. It won an Academy Award in 1955 for the best film song of the year.

Webster's experience proves that a writer should never give up on a song he or she believes can become an international hit. "The writing of words and music is an abstract art, so singers are often wrong on songs." Those who turned down "Love Is a Many-Splendored Thing" have been kicking themselves ever since.

Quality Songs Pay Off in the Long Run

Paul Webster has built a solid reputation as a writer of quality ballads. But because of this very fact, he had to rise above certain labels his work received: "All publishers want ballads, but because my songs were quality ballads, 'too pretty to be commercial' or 'way above the heads of the music-buying public' or 'too rangy' they were rejected. They were greeted with comments like 'why the minor key? Dirges don't sell,' or 'sixty-four-bar chorus? You must be kidding,' or 'who wants a waltz?' "

Yet look what happened. Webster's first international hit was 64 bars, another all-time best seller he wrote was in a minor key, another had an octave and five spread, while half dozen other hits from his pen were waltzes.

Webster remains convinced that quality songs will not only be accepted, but will pay off much greater in the long run: "Of one thing I am certain: the public will not only accept and buy quality songs and ballads, but will reward those possessed of quality with bigger sales and greater longevity than the cheap ditties that shoot up and down the charts like fireflies and disappear in the dawn. The only problem, and it's a big one, is how to get exposure on these so-called class songs."

That one word—quality—best sums up Webster the man and Webster the lyricist. The Webster song catalog is saturated with quality: "My Moonlight Madonna," "Memphis in June," "Loveliest Night of the Year," "I'll Walk With God," "A Very Precious Love," "The Twelfth of Never," "Secret Love," "I Speak to the Stars," "The Green Leaves of Summer," "Padre," "Giant," "Friendly Persuasion," "A Certain Smile," "April Love," "Tender Is the Night," "Somewhere, My Love," "The Shadow of Your Smile" (an Oscar winner) and "A Time for Love."

The Man Behind the Songs

Webster's comfortable study is filled with the tangible signs of a deeply intelligent man. At one end of his study is a picture of Webster taken with George Gershwin and a few other friends. The picture was taken just a week before Gershwin died of a brain tumor in 1937.

Above the framed picture is the manuscript of Julia Ward Howe's "Battle Hymn of the Republic." It's one of Webster's priceless posessions. One entire wall is covered with gold record awards, plaques, Grammies, and music publication citations attesting to Webster's brilliant career as a song lyricist. His three Oscars are very much present too.

The triumphs of this gentle and talented man continue each year. He got a standing ovation at Nashville's famed Country Music Festival recently when an award of outstanding merit was presented to him for his country-western standard, "Padre." His international hit, "Somewhere, My Love" (from "Doctor Zhivago") remained twelve weeks in the top ten. A country version of the song was recorded. His success in the country field proves that Webster's lyric talents are not limited to sophisticated, high quality film songs alone.

In answer to that old question of which comes first, the lyric or the tune, Webster usually works from the music first, but not always: "Hearing the music first suggests ideas, but it depends often on what the project is. In some shows, the lyric comes first. A studio sets the theme. On ballads, it's more effective with the melody first."

Songs That Were Tough to Write

Webster has received his share of tough film assignments during his career. These were songs that had to have the same title as the film. And some film titles can be particularly difficult to turn into songs. Those Paul remembers as being the hardest titles for him included "Man on Fire," "Invitation," "55 Days at Peking," "The Inn of the Sixth Happiness," and "The Guns of Navarone."

What can even a master lyricist do lyrically with a title like "Inn of the Sixth Happiness?" As Webster puts it, "Some film assignments present problems that take longer. Some are like jigsaw puzzles; others are good assignments. You write what you think the picture should have."

Some of the blues and jazz songs he wrote were troublesome too. One problem comedy song he did turned out great, "You Haven't Lived Til You Died in L. A." "The Shadow of Your Smile," his Academy Award winner in 1965, was also difficult. Webster was under some extra pressure and was competing with others while writing this one. He solved the lyric problem well, using specific words to denote sad and happy—"shadow" for sad and "smile" for happy.

Webster's own personal list of all-time favorite songs

includes great standards like "Smoke Gets in Your Eyes," "The Impossible Dream," "September Song," "When the World Was Young," "Old Man River," "It Was a Very Good Year," "Dancing in the Dark," "Camelot," and "Begin the Beguine."

Where does a writer like Webster do his work? Much of it is done in his study, but Webster misses the day of the trains. He liked to work on a train and felt very creative while riding on them. "I once wrote three songs on a train, while going back east with Sammy Fain. You could get up and walk around. Trains were romantic."

Songs He Enjoyed Writing Most

The songs that have given Webster the most pleasure in writing are "Friendly Persuasion," "Love Is a Many-Splendored Thing," "The Green Leaves of Summer," and "The Shadow of Your Smile." As for his largest seller, "Some songs do better in performances. Others are big in sheet music sales, like "I'll Walk With God." According to Herman Starr, head of Witmark Music Publishers, " 'I'll Walk with God' outsells in sheet music our three biggest copyrights: 'Tea for Two,' 'The Man I Love,' and 'Indian Love Call.' "

The Future of the Music Industry

What kind of future does Webster see for the music industry? "When the minstrel came to court and played, he wasn't really different from today's Joan Baez. There will be more and more experimenting with electronic effects, like that of John Cage. But ballads will still be around. We keep coming back to ballads."

Since winning his first Academy Award in 1953, Webster has seen the Oscar presentation for the best film songs become more competitive today with promotion. In a recent year there were over 300 eligible songs. With that competition it is a unique experience to hear your name called out three different times as the writer of the best film song of the year. Webster knows that feeling well: "With each successive award, it becomes an even greater incentive."

A Great Songwriter's Contribution

Webster's way with a lyric and his overall professionalism are highly admired and respected by his colleagues in the industry. His composer-collaborators have been delighted with the words he has given their music. His fellow writers have nothing but praise for him.

Jeane Dixon once said that "God weaves His tapestry, using history itself plus the lives and talents of many individuals." The unforgettable songs of Paul Francis Webster have been a significant part of that tapestry in our time—songs that have stirred our emotions, given us a lift, reminded us of the beautiful things in life, and lingered in the wings of our memories.

23

The Enduring Value of Evergreens

By now you should be aware of the enduring value of standards. Your chances of making a fortune as a songwriter will be far better if you can create the type of song that will be used and performed many times year after year.

What Is a Standard?

A standard is a song that gets recorded hundreds of times and is played on radio stations thousands of times all over the country. The songwriter who has a standard is like the prospector who hits oil. They both keep paying off for many years.

"The Shadow of Your Smile" is a standard. It was one of the most successful songs of the 1960s (released in 1965) and heard everywhere. But the point is that it's still being recorded today by many different artists on various labels. The song keeps popping up on new recordings and albums. It's also performed on national television programs.

"King of the Road" is a standard. It's been cut hundreds of times and performed many thousands of times on radio, television, and in nightclubs. Other songs that have become standards include "I Left My Heart in San Francisco," "Yesterday," "Moonlight Serenade," "Rose Garden," "Moon River," "Hello, Dolly," "For Once in My Life," "Misty," "Hello Young Lovers," and "If Ever I Would Leave You."

Almost any type of song can become a standard, if it's popular enough, and if it's a song that many people will love and continue to remember as the years go by. Novelty songs, ballads, country, rhythm and blues, jazz numbers, instrumentals, rock classics, and other material have all become standards.

One of the major reasons Lawrence Welk has been on television for over a quarter of a century is that he sticks to standard songs. His weekly show has consistently been one of the most successful on the tube. There must be a reason for this kind of success, and part of the reason is that he uses the songs that have lasted through the years. Millions of people never tire of hearing old standards like "Blue Skies," "Chicago," "Imagination," "In the Mood," "Tree in the Meadow," "Cab Driver," and hundreds of others.

Welk Says They're Writing Standards Again

The Lawrence Welk program format reflects the kind of music his viewers expect and like. He avoids many of the newer songs of recent years: "For a little while we couldn't even play a new song. We have to be very careful with the lyrics, just as we have to be very careful not to play too loud. But they're coming back to writing the standard songs. In making out our program for this tour, we used seven new songs. We used to be lucky to get one or two new songs. My audience is basically my age group, but last year we had more young people at our shows than ever before. We did this without losing our mother and father audience."

If you want to make millions as a songwriter, it should be clear to you that the best way to do this is to turn out songs that will live, be recorded, and performed thousands of times. That means standards. This is exactly what the top name writers are doing and will continue to do because they're aware of the money that can be made from standards.

Another good word for a standard is "evergreen." It means the same thing. "It Had to Be You," by Gus Kahn, is an evergreen. So are "You'll Never Know," "Laura," "Love Letters," "My Foolish Heart," "12th Street Rag," "Pretend," "Near You," "Young at Heart," and many others you can name yourself.

Story of an Evergreen

Years ago a man named J. Maloy Roach was attending a church service with his mother. She asked him to go down to light the candle. He asked himself if the world wouldn't be a better place, if every person lit a candle. He knew at that moment that he had a very strong song idea.

Sometime later Roach completed a song to his liking, with the help of a collaborator (George Mysels). He called his new song "One Little Candle."

J. Maloy Roach believed in his new song and began making the rounds of various music publishers. He was turned down time and again. He could have easily given up on the song and quit trying. But he had a strong conviction that "One Little Candle" would sell once the right company heard it. He eventually succeeded in bringing it to the attention of Fred Waring's music publishing firm. Once they had heard the song and realized its huge potential, they acted fast. The song was recorded by the Fred Waring musical group within several days after it was accepted.

"One Little Candle" went on to be recorded by Perry Como. A number of other artists recorded the song, and it was used in albums. An attractive sheet music edition was published, and even better, the world famous Christophers, a Catholic brotherhood organization, used the song as its theme. This meant that the song was performed every time the Christophers broadcast their series of programs.

The use of the song as a theme chalked up a lot of performances. By this time, the song had become a definite standard—an evergreen. It is still frequently heard today on radio, on television, and in new recorded versions. It has naturally been one of J. Maloy Roach's most successful songs and one he is very proud of.

Memories of Other Evergreens

There have been other songs that have made the charts and held their own in the musical spotlight for weeks or months. This is fine. These short-lived songs make money. They may not be up there for very long, but they earn well while they are. But it's the standards, the evergreen songs, that stick in my own memory and the memories of countless millions.

I still remember hearing the big evergreen tunes of the 1940s and 1950s. I was just a boy, but they still stand out in my mind. Some of these evergreens were "You'll Never Know" (from the old film, *Hello Frisco Hello*), Glenn Miller's unforgettable recordings of "Moonlight Serenade," "Pennsylvania 65000," "Little Brown Jug," and "The Serenade of the Bells." I used to dance at our school's teen canteen to a song called "Maybe You'll Be There." I still remember every word of the lyrics. These songs are like old friends to me today. Millions of others feel the same way.

Standards Are Worth the Extra Effort

To write the type of song that becomes a standard, an evergreen, may well take more time and effort. Standards aren't usually written in a few hours or days. A long series of rewrites may even be necessary. However, if you could turn out a few standards each year for a number of years, you could easily rise to the million-dollar bracket of songwriting success. There are far more songwriter millionaires than you might expect.

It does, however, take a number of years to tell if a song is going to reach the coveted plateau of a standard.

Standards may be written about any number of subjects. But to help and guide you to create standards, here are some major subjects that most people like to sing about or have sung to them:

1. Love. This is the most popular by far. Eighty percent of all popular songs up to the 1950s dealt with this subject.

2. Home. "The Green, Green Grass of Home," "Home Sweet Home," and "A House Is Not a Home" all did very nicely.

3. America. Patriotic numbers have become enormous standards. Some examples are "God Bless America," "America the Beautiful," "It's a Great Country," and "This Land Is Your Land."

4. Mother. This subject has to be handled carefully, but it has worked well before. How about "Mother Machree?" "Mama Sang a Song" did well in recent years.

Study the Great Standards

One definite way to increase your chances of creating more standards is simply to study the strong songs of today that appear to be headed toward the status of evergreens. You can pick your music field and examine the standards of each decade working your way back to the 1950s or earlier.

24

The Realness of Country Songs

There's a strong sense of reality in the country music today. Both in the content of the songs and in the conviction of the singers themselves. Country music says in effect: "This is how it is." If you decide to specialize in country songwriting, you need to keep this truth in mind and study the country hits.

Country singers are sincere. They believe in what they're singing, and this belief comes across in their recording and public appearances. This sincerity, blended with the realness of the lyrics, helps keep country music in continuing demand and favor. Songs like "Gentle on My Mind," "Phoenix," "For the Good Times," and others have the sound of life about them. For example, the song of some years back, "Detroit City," shows what has happened to a Southern man who's gone North to get a job.

How is this reality communicated to the listener? There's vivid identification in the lyrics. Country lyrics speak to the listener. People who listen to country records want to be able to identify with what the singer is experiencing and singing about.

Other communicators use this process of identification. Short story writers and novelists use it. Country lyrics are believable, down-to-earth lines that describe a situation, an experience, tell a story, or create a mood that seems real to the listener.

Sincerity Sells Country Music

Country songs reflect important values. The late Tex Ritter, one of the great country stars, said it well: "I don't think it's a matter of going back to the values of the past. I think it's a matter of going forward to the values of the future. They're the same values our forefathers knew, because the right values are eternal. That's one big reason for the swing back to country music by the nation as a whole. It's honest, and it's real, and its values are right."

Country songs stick in the minds of listeners because they reflect sincere attitudes regarding life, love, the family, marriage, work, travel, getting somewhere or not, history, religion, ideals or the lack of them, and standards of behavior.

Country star Minnie Pearl says it this way: "Country music is the music of the thinking working man, identified by its simple lyrics, easily understood, and its simple tunes, easily hummed."

The lyrics of country songs then meet life head on and tell about the feelings and emotions of people. The subject of love is treated in a nonpoetic way. "End of the World" and "Cold War with You" are two examples. Love is a very popular subject, but it's highlighted in language that is easily understood, "I'm Walkin' the Floor Over You" is an example.

Glen Campbell has said that in considering new material for recording he usually "looks for a song that tells a story." So, in a real sense, perhaps there's more entertainment value in country music.

When you think about it, country songs speak to all of us. Nearly everybody has similar problems. Many people are lonely or in love. So naturally the listener experiences the same problems that are recalled by the song. The listener can often identify with the story in the lyrics.

Country Songs Are More Sophisticated Today

Country songs are getting more sophisticated. Such songs as "For the Good Times," "You're the Best Thing That Ever Happened to Me," "I Won't Mention it Again" cross musical borders.

Evidently, a country song can be more sophisticated than some years back, while still being commercial and popular. This reveals a significant change that has taken place in the public in general. That change is a new demand for the truth, a desire for less fantasy and more realism. People want to know how things really are. Country music, which has helped bring about this change, deserves to be called one of the most popular art forms of modern times.

Many of the recordings of artist Ray Price have an overall sophisticated sound. Ray Price is a giant artist in the country field. His professional bearing and devotion to quality are legend. He's sung with small bands and symphony orchestras. Ray grew up in Dallas. When he launched his career, he was 100 percent country. Had it not been for the lure of performing, he would probably be a rancher or farmer today. He sang on the "Big D Jamboree" and first recorded on the Bullet label.

Price launched a new and unique sound in 1956, reflected in "I've Got a New Heartache" and "Crazy Arms." Since then, his special and unforgettable sound has been heard around the world. He never thought his style and sound had to be slipped into the industry: "I never felt I had to come in the back door." Instead, he blazed a fresh new trail in country music.

Uptown Country

Ray Price's records often cross musical borders. "For the Good Times" is one example. It broke all his previous records, crossing both country and pop borders. Price's style has been called "uptown country," as well as "smooth with velvet on the side."

Price is a remarkable singer. His voice wrings every shred of emotion out of a song. He believes in letting his audience and listeners hear each word of the song lyric. He's a master vocal craftsman who knows how to properly sustain a note and how to capture all the melody, emotion, and meaning of a song.

Hearing Ray Price sing "Danny Boy" is quite an experience. You can tell how much he loves this song by the compelling way he handles the phrasing. I have personally seen many crowds at Country Music Conventions leap to their feet and cheer until Price has sung the song again. As an artist, Ray Price has certainly brought quality into the country field.

The Country "Weeper"

The realness of country songs also means sad songs. "Born to Lose" is a good example. A breakdown of 350 songs, selected from a music publisher's catalog, revealed the following song catagories:

4 percent — western themes
5 percent — optimistic love songs
5 percent — sacred songs
1 percent — dance tunes

20 percent — miscellaneous
65 percent — sad love songs better known as "weepers"

Authorities and scholars who have studied the country field claim that there's a greater variety of subject matter in country songs. This might mean that more choice of subject matter is open to you in writing for the country field.

An examination of the past and current country song charts reveal that there are all types of country songs: divorce songs, work songs, songs about family finances and family troubles in general, triangle or infidelity songs, truck songs, moving to the city songs, parent-pride songs, poverty songs, and love songs (love being further broken down to include adultery, lost love, newly won love, tragic love affairs and humility).

So if you want to write country songs, strive to come up with a strong premise, then ask yourself if the topic is really down-to-earth. Keep it simple, and get a title that spotlights the whole idea behind the song. Use everyday language. Make your songs so real that they'll hit listeners where they live. Do all this and you just might have a hit.

25

Some Song Copyrights Are Worth Millions

Make no mistake about song copyrights. They can potentially be worth millions of dollars. There are heartbreaking stories of songwriters, in the early decades of the century, who sold all rights to their songs for flat fees. And the fees were usually next to nothing. Never sell your songs outright. They might just go on to make someone else a fortune.

Try to see both sides of the music business. Realize that there is a business side to songwriting, along with the creative side. Most of the songs you write may not be very good at first. But if you keep at it, over a period of time chances are that some of your songs will be real moneymakers.

Set up a safe place to keep your songs, song copyrights, contracts, and other business papers and correspondence. Many writers use filing cabinets. Try to be as businesslike as you can, for it will help you in your overall career.

The Song That Became a Christmas Annuity

You may not feel that your songs will go very far, but you just can't be sure. Remember, many writers are sometimes poor judges of their own songs. A song you write and copyright may possibly bring you a fortune years after you write it. Never knowing how far a given song might go is one thing that makes the songwriting game so exciting.

Composer-author J. Fred Coots, a 50-year veteran of the music business, has had over 700 songs published, including such big favorites as "Love Letters in the Sand," "For All We Know," "You Go to My Head," "I Still Get a Thrill," and "A Beautiful Lady in Blue."

Coots was born and grew up in Brooklyn. After showing an early interest in playing the piano and in writing music and lyrics, he launched his music career by landing a job as a song-plugger for a New York music firm. Coots had a short-lived Wall Street career working as a messenger, but the experience convinced him that the world of finance wasn't for him. From then on, he was determined to make his way as a songwriter.

One of his greatest hits, "Santa Claus Is Coming to Town," is still a Christmas season favorite year after year. Written in the 1930s, the song is the third biggest song seller in the history of Tin Pan Alley. In just 20 years the song sold 30 million records and more than four million sheet music copies.

Coots was playing the piano in his office one hot summer afternoon back in the 1930s. Haven Gillespie, a lyricist, came rushing into his office with some words he had written. Gillespie wanted Coots to look the words over and possibly do some music. Coots read the lines and asked what it was all about. Gillespie explained that it was a Christmas song for children. It was hard to think of Christmas songs on such a scorching day, but Coots began to see the potential of what Gillespie had written.

The more Coots thought about it, the more he liked the idea and the lyrics Gillespie had brought him. So he worked out some catchy music that fit the lyrics very well, and they had a new Christmas song ready for market.

So on a hot summer day, "Santa Claus Is Coming to Town" was born. The copyright on this song has been worth a fortune.

An annual Christmas bonanza, "Santa Claus Is Coming to Town" continues to sell well and is played a lot on stations all over the country every Yuletide season. It brings in a lot of performance rights money and has become a valuable yearly annuity for Coots.

For a number of years J. Fred Coots headed his own music publishing company, which he called Toy Town Tunes. His firm specialized in songs for children, and his many successes included "The Little Tin Soldier," "The Wedding of Jack and Jill," "Me and My Teddy Bear," and "Little Sally One-Shoe"—songs for children that have been gold mines. The copyrights on such songs are like personal treasures. And of course songs for children last for years.

In the course of his fabulous career, J. Fred Coots helped the careers of a number of famous people, including Bing Crosby, Kate Smith, Perry Como, Judy Garland, and Jackie Gleason. He also discovered the great Jimmy Durante playing piano in an unknown Harlem nightclub.

Coots collaborated with highly respected lyric writers on most of his songs, since he preferred to do the music. According to Coots, sometimes it takes time and many changes before a song comes together: "Some songs are mismated; you may have to wait to get the proper words and music together."

J. Fred Coots made his professional debut in the music world by playing piano in a downtown New York music store. From there he became a pianist and song promoter for a top music publishing company. Asked to write the songs for a Broadway show, *Sally, Irene and Mary,* Coots created a memorable score. The show was on Broadway for two years. The Shubert Brothers hired him soon afterward to do the music for many of their Broadway productions.

That Reindeer Named Rudolph

Another rich copyright since 1949 has been the yearly classic, "Rudolph the Red-Nosed Reindeer," another Christmas song written mainly for children. Some of the most valuable song copyrights are Christmas songs.

Johnny Marks wrote "Rudolph" back in the late 1940s and has been counting his millions ever since. The song has sold about 60 million records in America, over 27 million overseas, and millions more in sheet music copies. Mark is also the writer of other Christmas songs, including "I Heard the Bells on Christmas Day," "A Merry Merry Christmas," "The Night Before Christmas Song," "When Santa Claus Gets Your Letter," and "A Holly Jolly Christmas."

Important Questions You Need to Answer

It stands to reason that you need to decide which type of song market you feel you can most effectively write. Here are some questions to ask yourself.

1. Should I write for the bubble-gum market, that is the millions of teenagers? They buy a lot of records.

2. Do I want to write rock or popular songs for the youth market? Is this type of song where my strength lies as a writer?

3. Am I a country songwriter? Would I be more successful writing mostly sad songs that express regret over lost love, lost homes, lost chances, and other similar subjects?

4. Will I ignore the over-30 market, those who like ballads and songs with lasting appeal?

5. Am I the Broadway show tune writer? Would I be effective in writing songs for characters on a stage to sing, songs written around a certain situation?

6. Am I a folk song, blues, jazz, or gospel-sacred music songwriter?

7. Should I try to create a new Christmas or seasonal song and possibly concentrate on doing special songs? Songs for children, for example?

Keep in mind that millions of people over 30 buy an enormous number of records. Write for young people alone, and you miss this potentially gigantic market for your material. As music veteran Len Levy puts it, "A piece of material with strong melody and lyrics, like 'Love Story' has broad and lasting appeal. On the whole, too many record people have lost sight of the broad spectrum of the American public, which can be reached by strong melodic lines and good lyrics. Music people are overlooking the subteen and over 30-markets."

Your Songwriting Time Is Valuable

The song copyrights that may be in your name some day in the future could be worth a great deal of money to you. You should go over the songs you've written once or twice a year and try to choose the ones you feel are the most valuable. Then do your utmost to get those songs placed.

When he was asked for a patriotic song, Irving Berlin took "God Bless America" from his files. He had written it many years earlier. Never fail to go over material you haven't yet placed. The demand for certain types of songs changes. You may find just the right song for a market or artist in your files.

You may want to decide on a definite number of songs

to write for a year, or so many songs per week or month. Comedian, songwriter, and musician Steve Allen has a goal of three new songs a week. He makes his time count, often working well into the early morning hours on songs, books, comedy routines, and other creative projects.

One of the most important things you have going for you as a songwriter is time itself. Many songwriters who are in the business full-time keep regular office hours. They put in eight or more hours five or six days a week. Some of them claim that this attitude has helped them to produce valuable song copyrights.

In Margaret Mitchell's unforgettable novel, *Gone With the Wind*, a sign at the plantation home of John Wilkes said it all: "Do not squander time . . .. for that is the stuff life is made of." There are millions of people across the land who would love to have the time to follow their songwriting interests more closely. Instead most of their time is spent in making a living. So use your time wisely, and you'll have more song copyrights to offer.

Whether you write songs part-time or full-time, here are some useful tips on getting more out of your writing time. The creative process cannot be forced, but you may be able to accomplish more by using some of these suggestions:

1. Don't waste all your weekends. You naturally want and deserve to take some time off. But if the creative juices start flowing on Saturday morning, go to it. You may turn out a hit.

2. Try to make a point of doing first things first. Do the important items on your list first and the rest as your time allows.

3. Get up an hour earlier. You may find it difficult the first week or so. But then you may find yourself eager to get up and make that extra hour or so really count. You can train yourself to write at any time.

4. Work on your songs an hour or two later at night.

Many writers find that they work best at such times. It's quieter and easier to think late at night. Cole Porter did much of his best work in the late hours.

5. Make your lunch hours count. If you're lunching alone, you can at least think about a lyric line or a new song idea you like. You can jot down notes after lunch.

26

Songwriting—Fascinating Leisure-time Activity

It's rewarding when the songs you write make money, climb the charts, sell in the record racks and stores, are played often on radio stations, and bring you national publicity as a hit songwriter. It's very possible to make a million dollars and more from your songs. But aside from the always present chance to make some real money, songwriting itself makes a fascinating leisure-time activity.

No songwriter has a written guarantee that his or her songs will make money. You do your best on each song and then go on to the next one. But the truth is that songwriting is also a lot of fun.

Why Songwriting Makes a Great Hobby

There are some clear reasons why songwriting offers you an ideal leisure-time pursuit. One real advantage is the fact that you can work on songs just about anywhere and anytime. While you're standing in one of life's many lines, you can be thinking about a lyric. I've worked on lyrics and tunes in my mind while flying on planes, attending boring meetings or seminars, or taking a stroll.

Although a piano or guitar can help, the actual creation of songs goes on in the mind. If you can't get to a piano or guitar when ideas hit you, it's possible to carry a small recorder with you and tape yourself humming or singing your tune fragment. A notebook and pen are all you need for certain, if you're basically a lyric writer.

Songwriting is an excellent way to practice creative expression. There's nothing like creative activity to keep you enthusiastic, happy, and really interested in every single day. Brooks Atkinson, the famous drama critic, once said that "every man can achieve a great deal according to the burning intensity of his will and the keenness of his imagination."

Before his death, Earle Stanley Gardner, the creator of Perry Mason, was still dictating up to 10,000 words a day and working on as many as seven novels at the same time. Of course, he had a staff of secretaries and assistants to help him.

When you write songs over a period of time, you also gain a definite sense of accomplishment. Even if nobody else hears them they can still be a source of pleasure for you. As their creator, you have given birth to them. That in itself is accomplishment.

Another positive factor about songwriting is that it could be a better investment in the long run than the stock market, coin collecting, lottery tickets, bonds, art, and other investments. It's entirely possible that a song you may write today, tomorrow, or next summer will succeed and bring you a fortune. This knowledge can fill you with strong incentive to grow and develop as a songwriter.

A real songwriter never gets tired of writing songs. It's the continuous sense of new ideas, new tunes kicking around in your head that nobody else has ever heard before, and the way many songs capture your attention that add freshness and challenge to each new song idea you develop into a complete song.

Let's face it. Songwriting is just plain fun, much the way playing Monopoly, or chess, or checkers is for millions of others. The day I wrote my first song lyric in the New York Public Library, shortly before leaving on an eight-month naval cruise, I knew I was hooked on songwriting for life. I worked all afternoon on the lyrics, but I had a ball that rainy afternoon in the big town. I discovered how much pleasure there is in writing a song. Even the troublesome songs that don't work out as one would hope still seem like fun when looked back on.

Take Pride in Being a Songwriter

Still another plus of the songwriter's way of life is pride. An increasing number of people around the world are realizing that having a sense of pride in what they do is important to their happiness, and a songwriter has a right to be proud.

Why is it that some people will work harder for praise than anything else? Because they need this feeling of pride of work well done.

A western gold prospector was recently interviewed on television. Now in his seventies, he's still doing his thing. He still enjoys looking for gold after so many years, and he's still proud to say that he's a prospector. Asked why he didn't quit and move back to some town where he could live more comfortably in his older years, he said that he'd never found anything he liked better than prospecting: "I'd be a prospector again, if I had my life to live over."

Humphrey Bogart, the unforgettable actor, was proud to be an actor: "I am a professional. I have a respect for my profession. I worked hard at it."

Walter Pidgeon, another highly respected performer, remained loyal to the film industry. In his late sixties he was still proud to call himself a motion picture actor: "I'm a movie man and a stage actor. Motion pictures still have a decent pace, not too fast for an old guy like me."

Andrew Jackson was just as proud to call himself a farmer as he had been as the nation's leader in the White House. He got enormous satisfaction from raising horses at his home outside Nashville.

Pride in your songwriting is important. It's healthy, stimulating, cleansing, and it goes a long way in helping you stand out from the crowd. Most people who are proud of what they do are usually successful at it; some are very successful. Being proud of your songwriting can help you become a better writer

Songwriting Brings New Friends and Meetings

Your interest in songwriting can bring you new friends who share the same interest in music. You're bound to make new acquaintances when you visit recording centers, seminars on songwriting, or music conventions. Once you have at least one song credit to your name, you can attend the regular business meetings of either ASCAP or BMI, whichever you decide to join.

The first ASCAP meeting I attended in the 1960s fascinated me. It was held in Hollywood. After the business was completed, a number of long tables were loaded with all kinds of food and refreshments for the members, and I met several name writers who were there for the meeting. I have since attended several ASCAP meetings in Nashville. The New York meetings are usually held at the Waldorf-Astoria.

The Chance to Grow

The majority of songwriters start out green and have a lot

to learn about the music business. After they have been writing for several years, they look back at the first songs they wrote. When they compare those early songs with the latest ones, they are amazed to see how much better and more professional their current songs are. It proves that they are growing and getting to be stronger writers.

Experts who have made a study of success and its principles say that a major reason millions of Americans don't attain real success is that they don't know precisely what they want to achieve; they don't have a clearly defined objective.

A physical education teacher I know loved golf more than anything else. At the end of each school day he would take off fast to get in a few hours of driving practice before the sun went down. He had known for years that what he wanted most was to be a pro golfer, but he hadn't started playing the game soon enough. "I didn't start playing golf til my late teens. To become a pro, and really have a chance you need to start playing by age seven or eight." Now in his mid-thirties, he's good at the game, but not good enough to make it as a professional.

One of the beauties of songwriting is that you don't have to start at age five or six (although that would probably give one a great head start). Some of the best songwriters didn't even begin writing til their late twenties or early thirties. And people who started much older have made a lot of money from their songs. Many have not realized their strong interest in music and songwriting until they were in their middle years. Young or old, it's never too early or too late to write that song in your heart. The next hit could come from you. Remember, the long established writers don't have a corner on fresh new song ideas. It's what you do with those song ideas that counts.

Singer and actress Julie Andrews voiced a great truth in her popular film, *The Sound of Music*. You can't take each day as it comes, hoping against hope that you'll fall into the right work through sheer luck. As Julie put it in the film "You have to look for your life."

According to Dr. Wallace Gobetz, director of the New York University Testing and Advisement Center, "More than half of us select a lifework almost accidentally without knowledge of ourselves or of the world of work."

If you're still in your student days or even your early twenties, now is the time to plan your future in songwriting, part-time or full-time. Look for clues while you're still in school that music and songwriting may be for you. The quicker you can find the field where you belong, the sooner you can start heading for your goal.

Songwriting Moonlighters

If you're older and can only follow your songwriting interest part-time, welcome the chance to be a songwriting moonlighter. The U. S. Department of Labor says there are over 21,700 different moneymaking vocations in the country today. Millions are moonlighting at one or more jobs.

A middle-aged Kentucky teacher I know is earning more as a part-time confession-story writer than he makes as a teacher. Every weekday evening, he fortifies himself with a good meal and hits the typewriter, sometimes knocking out two juicy confession yarns a week. All of them don't sell, of course, but a lot of them do.

An Indiana college professor picks up an extra $10,000 a year doing horoscopes for friends, students, neighbors, and people who see his ads. He says that the work fits in nicely with his college teaching and also gives him a fascinating sideline.

With an increasing number of companies and firms adopting a four-day work week, more and more workers have three other days and nights to work at a second or third job. Songwriting could certainly be one of these extra pursuits. It's better to have lots of time for it, but some time spent on it is better than nothing. You can certainly make some progress in your songwriting by moonlighting.

A number of people from various backgrounds have found a whole new world of opportunity opening up to them after months or years of moonlighting activity. Many of today's full-time, established songwriters started as part-timers or moonlighters.

One thing is certain. As a working songwriter, you'll never be bored. You'll be anxious to leave your regular work at the end of the day to turn to your songwriting activity. You will also feel the excitement of knowing that you might one day create a hit. Who knows what the future might have in store for you? I've been a songwriter for 20 years. Every day is a new adventure. There's nothing else like it.

Part-time or full-time, songwriters have more fun. See you out there in the wonderful world of songwriting—and many hits to you!

Appendix: Checklist for More Successful Songwriting

1. Write and work on new songs every week.
2. Write for the market of today.
3. Submit only complete songs.
4. Write a lot of songs every year so the law of averages will work for you.
5. Keep a master notebook of ideas for new songs and continually add to it. Refer to it often.
6. Use demo tapes to demonstrate and help sell your songs.
7. Keep your songs as simple as possible.
8. Remember that songwriting is a craft as well as an art. It's also a business.
9. Think seriously about specializing in either lyrics or music, unless you're convinced you can do both well.
10. Realize that old songs can be rewritten into hits. Be willing to change and rewrite your material to strengthen it.

11. Visit the major recording centers whenever you can and try to develop a growing list of contacts.

12. If you write only lyrics or music, find one or more collaborators you can work well with on new songs.

13. When you contact publishers, take a lead sheet and the typed lyrics of your song along with a demo.

14. Meet the talented singers in your city or town and urge them to use some of your songs. Offer to do new songs for any musical groups in your area.

15. Contact recording artists about your songs, personally, by mail, or through others.

16. Be constantly alert for strong new song titles.

17. Never send your songs out cold to a music publisher or record label. Contact them first, preferably in person, by letter or phone for their permission.

18. Try hard to match the right song with the right publisher. In other words, don't send a country song to a show tune publisher.

19. Obtain a Library of Congress copyright on the songs you feel are your strongest and most commercial. Keep the copyright certificates in a safe place.

20. Protect your other songs by registered mail, notes on when you started and completed them, and signatures of witnesses attesting to the fact that you are the creator of the material.

21. Try to write lyrics that are realistic and fresh.

22. Don't write songs that are too long. You want them to be played by disc jockeys when they've been recorded.

23. Strive to get emotional impact into your lyrics and music.

24. Keep your lyrics clean. You can be honest without being dirty. Clean songs last longer and can be performed before any type of audience.

25. Very simple songs can have a tremendous effect.

26. Realize that a song contract means little to a song-

writer until the song is actually recorded and released. Go after recordings of your songs.

27. Try to create music and melodies that are easy to remember.

28. Keep in mind that nightclub entertainers are often on the lookout for fresh material.

29. Attend seminars on songwriting whenever possible.

30. Read *Billboard, Cash Box,* and other leading music trade publications regularly. Stay well informed on what's happening in the industry.

31. Try writing material for different song categories such as pop, country, rhythm and blues, easy listening, show tunes, gospel, and the rest. Decide whether to specialize in one or more areas.

32. Definitely join either ASCAP or BMI, as soon as you have one song credit to your name.

33. Realize that many recording artists like lyrics that tell a basic story. Glen Campbell is one such artist.

34. Attend any and all music conventions whenever possible. Try to meet other writers, and artists, musicians, publishers, and recording executives.

35. Keep writing.

36. Read everything. Reading stimulates the mind.

37. Watch for new song ideas that are right for you.

38. Think positively about your songwriting at all times.

39. Experiment on the piano or guitar when you are trying to set lyrics to music. Play different chords. Be alert for motives (short 4-note kernels of melody) and melodic phrases.

40. Test an idea, lyric, or tune by setting it aside for several days and forgetting it. See if it keeps popping into your mind.

41. Try writing the last line of a lyric first and then working your way back to the beginning.

42. If you feel uncomfortable trying to write music down, hum or sing your tune on tape and then pay a musician, arranger, or music teacher a fee to make a lead sheet for you.

43. Never stop trying to place your songs. The very essence of creative ability is to keep trying harder.

44. Read and study the published lyrics in song magazines sold each month on newsstands. These are songs that are being recorded.

45. Promote your songs both before and after they are recorded.

46. Remember that persistence can be the most valuable and important quality in getting a hit song. Never, never give up.

47. Consider the idea of turning musician or performer yourself. Form your own musical group. If successful you have an ideal outlet for your songs.

48. Think about becoming a radio announcer or disc jockey. This can be a way into the music business. Many names of today got started this way.

49. Move to one of the major recording centers when your career starts to move, but be sure you have enough savings to last you a year or two.

50. Keep writing . . . keep writing . . . keep writing.

Index